SHAPING
THE DEFENSE CIVILIAN WORK FORCE

Studies in Defense Policy
TITLES IN PRINT

Support Costs in the Defense Budget: The Submerged One-Third
Martin Binkin

The Changing Soviet Navy
Barry M. Blechman

Strategic Forces: Issues for the Mid-Seventies
Alton H. Quanbeck and Barry M. Blechman

U.S. Reserve Forces: The Problem of the Weekend Warrior
Martin Binkin

U.S. Force Structure in NATO: An Alternative
Richard D. Lawrence and Jeffrey Record

U.S. Tactical Air Power: Missions, Forces, and Costs
William D. White

U.S. Nuclear Weapons in Europe: Issues and Alternatives
Jeffrey Record with the assistance of Thomas I. Anderson

The Control of Naval Armaments: Prospects and Possibilities
Barry M. Blechman

Stresses in U.S.-Japanese Security Relations
Fred Greene

The Military Pay Muddle
Martin Binkin

Sizing Up the Soviet Army
Jeffrey Record

Modernizing the Strategic Bomber Force: Why and How
Alton H. Quanbeck and Archie L. Wood
with the assistance of Louisa Thoron

Where Does the Marine Corps Go from Here?
Martin Binkin and Jeffrey Record

Deterrence and Defense in Korea: The Role of U.S. Forces
Ralph N. Clough

Women and the Military
Martin Binkin and Shirley J. Bach

The Soviet Military Buildup and U.S. Defense Spending
Barry M. Blechman and others

Soviet Air Power in Transition
Robert P. Berman

*Shaping the Defense Civilian Work Force: Economics,
Politics, and National Security*
Martin Binkin with Herschel Kanter and Rolf H. Clark

MARTIN BINKIN *with Herschel Kanter and Rolf H. Clark*

SHAPING
THE DEFENSE CIVILIAN WORK FORCE
Economics, Politics, and National Security

THE BROOKINGS INSTITUTION
Washington, D.C.

Library of Congress Cataloging in Publication Data:

Binkin, Martin   1928–
    Shaping the defense civilian work force.

    (Studies in defense policy; 19)
    Includes bibliographical references.
    1. United States.   Dept. of Defense—Officials
and employees.   2. United States.   Dept. of
Defense—Personnel management.   I. Kanter,
Herschel, joint author.   II. Clark, Rolf H., joint
author.   III. Title.   IV. Series.
UB193.B56   1978   355.6′1′0973   78-14897
ISBN 0-8157-0967-6

9 8 7 6 5 4 3 2 1

THE BROOKINGS INSTITUTION is an independent organization devoted to nonpartisan research, education, and publication in economics, government, foreign policy, and the social sciences generally. Its principal purposes are to aid in the development of sound public policies and to promote public understanding of issues of national importance.

The Institution was founded on December 8, 1927, to merge the activities of the Institute for Government Research, founded in 1916, the Institute of Economics, founded in 1922, and the Robert Brookings Graduate School of Economics and Government, founded in 1924.

The Board of Trustees is responsible for the general administration of the Institution, while the immediate direction of the policies, program, and staff is vested in the President, assisted by an advisory committee of the officers and staff. The by-laws of the Institution state: "It is the function of the Trustees to make possible the conduct of scientific research, and publication, under the most favorable conditions, and to safeguard the independence of the research staff in the pursuit of their studies and in the publication of the results of such studies. It is not a part of their function to determine, control, or influence the conduct of particular investigations or the conclusions reached."

The President bears final responsibility for the decision to publish a manuscript as a Brookings book. In reaching his judgment on the competence, accuracy, and objectivity of each study, the President is advised by the director of the appropriate research program and weighs the views of a panel of expert outside readers who report to him in confidence on the quality of the work. Publication of a work signifies that it is deemed a competent treatment worthy of public consideration but does not imply endorsement of conclusions or recommendations.

The Institution maintains its position of neutrality on issues of public policy in order to safeguard the intellectual freedom of the staff. Hence interpretations or conclusions in Brookings publications should be understood to be solely those of the authors and should not be attributed to the Institution, to its trustees, officers, or other staff members, or to the organizations that support its research.

FOREWORD

In recent years, as the Pentagon's budget has been squeezed between rising costs and alternative demands for federal funds, the defense payroll, which now amounts to roughly half of all defense spending, has come under close scrutiny. For the most part, however, attention has focused on the man in uniform, rather than on his civilian coworker in the military establishment.

This book, the nineteenth Brookings study in defense policy, is the first step in an analysis of the million-member defense civilian work force. Martin Binkin and his collaborators discuss the bureaucratic and political factors that now tend to muffle debate and discourage technical assessment. The authors query whether some of the jobs that defense civilians do have to be done at all and, if so, whether employing federal civilians is the best way to get them done. But they also ask whether it would be more efficient to substitute civilians, either government or private-sector employees, for military personnel.

The authors' main purposes are to provide the bases and rationale for change, to recommend procedures that would make it easier to strike the right balance between civilian and military defense manpower, and to propose an agenda for further research.

An earlier version of this study was published in September 1977 by the Committee on Armed Services of the U.S. Senate. The data have been updated and the text revised to reflect recent developments.

Martin Binkin, a senior fellow in the Brookings Foreign Policy Studies program, has written extensively on defense manpower issues. Herschel Kanter, also a Brookings senior fellow, is a contributor to *Setting National Priorities: The 1979 Budget* (Brookings, 1978). Commander Rolf H. Clark, who has since returned to active duty with the U.S. Navy, was a 1977–78 Brookings Federal Executive Fellow.

vii

The book has greatly benefited from the comments of William K. Brehm, General Bruce Palmer, Jr., and Robert Taft, Jr., who are members of the Brookings Defense Analysis Advisory Board. Numerous officials in the Office of the Secretary of Defense and in the military services provided data and assistance. The authors are particularly indebted to the staff of the Assistant Secretary of Defense (Manpower, Reserve Affairs, and Logistics) and to the Defense Manpower Data Center. They thank those who commented on drafts of the manuscript, especially Walter B. Bergmann II, Charles W. Groover, Clifford J. Miller, Richard F. Powers, Michael G. Sovereign, and Thomas M. Stanners.

They are also grateful to their former Brookings colleagues Barry M. Blechman and Henry Owen for valuable suggestions, to Barbara P. Haskins for editing the manuscript, to Judy Conmy for ensuring the accuracy of the data presented, and to Ann M. Ziegler and Georgina S. Hernandez, who shared the secretarial burden.

The Institution acknowledges the assistance of the Ford Foundation, whose grant helps to support its work in defense studies. The views expressed here are those of the authors and should not be ascribed to the persons who provided data or who commented on the manuscript, to the Senate Armed Services Committee, to the Ford Foundation, or to the trustees, officers, or other staff members of the Brookings Institution.

BRUCE K. MACLAURY
President

July 1978
Washington, D.C.

CONTENTS

1. **Introduction**   1

2. **The Civilian Work Force Today**   3
   Guidelines Governing the Use of Civilians *5*
   Civilian Jobs in the Defense Establishment *7*
   Cost of Defense Civilian Manpower *9*

3. **Shapers of Defense Manpower Policy: Bureaucrats and Politicians** 15
   Bureaucratic Interests *15*
   Domestic Politics *19*

4. **Efficiencies in the Use of Civilian Manpower**   26
   Base Operations Support *26*
   The Logistics Establishment *33*

5. **The Military-Civilian Mix**   42
   Comparing the Costs of Military and Civilian Manpower *42*
   Potential Utilization under Current Policies *52*
   Potential Utilization under Revised Policies *57*

6. **Government or Private Enterprise?**   61
   Relative Costs of In-House and Private Contractor Operations *61*
   Further Opportunities *66*

7. **Shaping the Defense Civilian Work Force: Conclusions and
   Recommendations**   71
   General Conclusions *72*
   Encouraging Reform *74*

   Appendixes
   A. Composition of the Defense Civilian Work Force *85*
   B. How Decisions Are Made on Civilian Manpower *91*
   C. Cost Derivations *96*

Tables

2-1. Defense Civilian Employment, Averages for Selected
Fiscal Years 1945–78   4

2-2. U.S. Direct Hire Civilian Employees, by Occupational Group,
September 1977   8

2-3. Distribution of Defense Civilian Manpower, by Defense Planning
and Programming Categories, Fiscal Years 1964 and 1978   9

2-4. Projected Defense Civilian Payroll Costs, by Employment
Category, Fiscal Year 1978   10

2-5. Average Defense Civilian Per Capita Payroll Costs, by Category
of Employment, Fiscal Years 1968 and 1978   11

2-6. Comparison of Night Shift Differential Rates for Private-Sector
and Federal Employees, Five Selected Areas, 1976   13

4-1. Trends in Defense Manpower, Fiscal Years 1975 and 1978   28

4-2. Base Operations Support and Mission Manpower, Selected
Air Force Bases with Strategic Air Mission, June 1975   32

4-3. Ship Overhaul Costs, Selected Fiscal Years 1968–78   35

4-4. Indexes of Overhead and Man-Day Costs, Selected Naval
Shipyards, Fiscal Year 1976   39

5-1. Average Annual Compensation Costs for Selected Military
and Civilian Grades, Fiscal Year 1978   45

5-2. Average Annual Pipeline Costs for Selected Military and Civilian
Grades, Fiscal Year 1978   46

5-3. Average Annual Indirect Support Costs for Selected Military
and Civilian Grades, Fiscal Year 1978   47

5-4. Comparison of Median Job Content between Military Personnel
and Federal Civilian Employees at Selected Grade Levels   48

5-5. Total Average Annual Costs Attributable to Selected Military
Grades and Equivalent Federal Civilian Grades, September 1977   49

5-6. Maximum Potential Substitution of Civilian for Military Enlisted
Billets, by Service, Fiscal Year 1977   56

6-1. Number of Man-Years Spent on Commercial and Industrial
Activities by In-House and Contract Personnel,
Department of Defense, Fiscal Year 1975   67

6-2. In-House Commercial and Industrial Activities, by Service,
Fiscal Year 1975   68

A-1. Comparison of Projected Civilian and Military Personnel
Strength in the Department of Defense, End of
Fiscal Year 1978   86

A-2. Projected Distribution of Defense Civilians, End of
Fiscal Year 1978   87

A-3. Civilian Employees by Type, by Geographical Region, December 1976   87

A-4. U.S. Direct Hire Civilian Employees by Major Occupational Group and by Functional Area, September 1977   88

A-5. Distribution of Military Personnel and Equivalent Full-Time Federal Civilians in Enlisted-Level Positions, Department of Defense, September 1977   89

C-1. Estimated Average Annual Compensation-related Costs, Military Personnel, by Grade, 1978   97

C-2. Estimated Average Annual Compensation-related Costs, General Schedule Civilians, by Grade, 1978   98

C-3. Estimated Average Annual Compensation-related Costs, Wage Board (Supervisor) Civilians, by Grade, 1978   99

C-4. Estimated Average Annual Compensation-related Costs, Wage Board (Leader) Civilians, by Grade, 1978   100

C-5. Estimated Average Annual Compensation-related Costs, Wage Board (Nonsupervisor) Civilians, by Grade, 1978   101

C-6. Estimated Average Annual Pipeline Costs, Military Personnel, by Grade, 1978   104

C-7. Estimated Average Annual Pipeline Costs, General Schedule Civilians, by Grade, 1978   105

C-8. Estimated Annual Pipeline Costs, Wage Board Civilians, by Category and Grade, 1978   106

C-9. Estimated Average Annual Support Costs, Military and Civilian Personnel, by Grade, 1978   107

C-10. Estimated Average Total Costs by Grade, 1978   108

C-11. Comparison of High, Median, and Low Estimates of Job Content between Military Personnel and Federal Civilian Employees at Selected Grade Levels   110

C-12. Estimated Median Military Costs Relative to High, Median, and Low Estimates for Equivalent Civilian Grades, 1978   112

CHAPTER ONE

INTRODUCTION

Federal civilian employees have been associated with the military establishment since the early nineteenth century and have constituted at least 20 percent of total defense manpower since World War I. The proportion is now over 30 percent—about 1 million employees—and yet it remains one of the least understood components of the U.S. defense establishment.

Assessing the defense civilian work force in general and evaluating the respective national defense roles of military, federal civilian, and private-sector employees, in particular, have probably never been so important as they are today. Although the sharp increase in the real cost of defense manpower that occurred in the early 1970s has been largely brought under control, the manpower component of the Pentagon's budget continues to be an important consideration among policymakers apprehensive about the recent Soviet military buildup. The degree to which efforts to match or offset improvements in Soviet military power increase the financial burden of defense will depend largely on how efficiently U.S. defense resources are managed; controlling manpower costs will be an essential element in any such program. Also, growing doubts about whether this nation will be able to sustain an all-volunteer force of appropriate quality accentuate the need to evaluate possible substitutes for military manpower, and hence bring the potential roles of defense civilians and private-sector workers into even sharper focus.

Accordingly, two principal questions are addressed in this study:

1. Are the jobs that defense civilians are now doing essential and, if so, is employing defense civilians the most efficient way to get them done?

2. Should the nation rely to a greater extent on civilians, either in the government or the private sector, to do some of the jobs now being done by military personnel?

The study concludes that defense payroll costs are higher than necessary. Many defense civilian employees are being paid in excess of an appropriate market wage; some jobs being done by defense civilians cannot be justified in national security terms; other positions filled by military incumbents could be filled more efficiently by federal civilians; and some tasks carried out by government employees—either military or federal civilian—could be accomplished more efficiently through contractual arrangements with private industry.

It is impossible to predict with precision the number of jobs in excess of military requirements or the extent to which the composition of the defense labor force can be shifted without undue risk. Indeed, the principal purpose here is not to estimate the magnitude of possible changes; that task requires a more detailed analysis for which the Pentagon will have to collect a good deal more information. Rather the purpose is to examine and explain why any change is necessary, recommend how it might be brought about so as to make more effective use of manpower resources, and to expose those areas of analysis where further investigation and research are urgently needed.

Pushing the analysis as far as available data permit, the study is but a first step in the long overdue examination of the appropriate mix of military, federal civilian, and private-sector workers employed by the defense establishment. The next steps, as advocated in the study, are up to Congress, the White House, and the Pentagon.

CHAPTER TWO

THE CIVILIAN WORK FORCE TODAY

The Department of Defense has the largest work force of any single U.S. government agency or private enterprise.[1] Of the 3 million or so people employed 1 million are civilians, doing 1,520 different sorts of jobs in a wide variety of military organizations both at home and abroad. There are some 570,000 white-collar and 330,000 blue-collar workers, and also 120,000 foreign nationals employed abroad either directly or through arrangements with host countries. The payroll exceeds $18 billion, or about 17 percent of total defense spending.[2] Despite changing trends caused by war and conscription, table 2-1 shows that the proportion of civilians to uniformed personnel has always been high—roughly one-third since 1950.

The Pentagon also estimates that, through contracts with industry, it generates employment for another 2 million civilian workers in the private sector.[3] An estimated 130,000 of these people are engaged in so-called commercial and industrial activities, including equipment maintenance, installation services, automatic data processing, and the like.[4]

What guidelines have governed the employment of this impressive number of people? What do they actually do, and what do they cost?

1. Its nearest rival, the American Telephone and Telegraph Company has about 927,000 employees. The second largest government organization (actually a quasi-official agency) is the U.S. Postal Service, which employs about 684,000 people.

2. Fiscal 1978 data. The composition of the civilian work force and a description of its various components is given in appendix A.

3. Department of Defense, "National Defense Budget Estimates for FY 1979" (1978; processed), p. 104.

4. About 370,000 defense employees are also employed in these activities, which are largely in logistics and base operating support. See *Contracting Out of Defense Functions and Services,* Hearing before the Subcommittee on Manpower and Personnel, Senate Armed Services Committee, 95:1 (Government Printing Office, 1977), pp. 60–63.

Table 2-1. Defense Civilian Employment, Averages for Selected Fiscal Years 1945–78[a]
Thousands of employees

Category[b]	1945	1950	1955	1960	1965	1970	1975	1978
Direct hire								
General schedule	921.1	318.0	486.4	489.2	525.7	637.2	586.1	566.6
Wage Board	1,445.7	402.7	621.9	505.9	439.9	455.5	365.3	328.5
Foreign national	67.2	51.2	97.7	72.0	64.4	137.4	46.9	36.7
Indirect hire								
Foreign national	250.1	190.6	363.6	183.2	135.4	104.4	85.9	81.0
Total civilian employment	2,684.1	962.6	1,569.6	1,250.2	1,165.4	1,334.5	1,084.2	1,012.8
Total military employment	11,809.1	1,538.8	3,177.8	2,489.4	2,665.8	3,293.5	2,146.6	2,066.3
Civilians as percentage of total	*18.5*	*38.5*	*33.1*	*33.4*	*30.4*	*28.8*	*33.6*	*32.9*

Source: Data provided by the Office of the Assistant Secretary of Defense (Comptroller), March 1978.
a. Actual data are shown for all fiscal years except 1978, which reflects the average number of employees for fiscal 1978 in the fiscal 1979 budget request.
b. See appendix A for explanation of categories.

These are important questions addressed below before an analysis of possible personnel, cost, and efficiency changes.

Guidelines Governing the Use of Civilians

The secretary of defense has provided fairly broad general directives for the military departments:

Civilian personnel will be used in positions which do not require military incumbents for reasons of law, training, security, discipline, rotation, or combat readiness, which do not require a military background for successful performance of the duties involved, and which do not entail unusual hours not normally associated or compatible with civilian employment.[5]

This basic policy extends to jobs in foreign countries as well. The 1954 directive also specified that "indigenous personnel will be utilized to the maximum extent practicable consistent with security and the necessity of maintaining a high state of readiness."[6]

Each of the services has established regulations to amplify the general directives, and because of their vague contours each has had wide discretion in defining the criteria to be applied in determining whether or not a position is to be filled with uniformed personnel. The Air Force, for example, specifies that military personnel will be used:

(1) In a unit/position directly engaged in combat functions, and in direct combat support functions.

(2) In a position that requires the exercise of command control, military training and discipline and which, by law, must be exercised by military personnel.

(3) In a unit that has combat mobility requirements.

(4) In a position in which military personnel must gain experience before they can assume responsibility for a combat function.

(5) In a position that requires certain skills and knowledge acquired primarily through military training.

(6) In a position where, to properly discharge its duties, a civilian incumbent would be forced to compromise his legal rights and privileges, or would be required to take action restricted by law to military personnel.

5. Department of Defense, Directive 1100.4, "Guidance for Manpower Programs," August 20, 1954, p. 2. A later directive, affirming this basic policy, omits reference to the "unusual hours" criterion. See Department of Defense, Directive 1400.5, "Statement of Personnel Policy for Civilian Personnel in the Department of Defense," January 16, 1970, p. 2.

6. Directive 1100.4, "Guidance for Manpower Programs."

(7) In a position in any area or grade, as necessary, to allow for normal career progression, and to support the CONUS overseas rotation prescribed by HQ USAF.

(8) In a position that is ordinarily filled by an in-service civilian, when no civilian manpower authorization/skills are available.[7]

For certain positions not considered to require a military incumbent, the services are confronted with a further choice: whether to fill the billet with a civil service employee or to contract for the services. Here, the official guidance reflects a prejudice toward contracting for services. The armed forces are guided by "the Government's general policy of relying upon the private enterprise system to supply its needs for products and services, in preference to engaging in [its own] commercial or industrial activity."[8]

The Department of Defense directive on the subject follows this guidance, specifying that certain activities that produce goods or services similar to those available in the private sector (defined as "commercial or industrial activities") may be continued in operation or initiated only for one or more of the following reasons:

a. Procurement of a product or service from a commercial source would disrupt or materially delay an agency's program.

b. It is necessary for the Government to conduct a commercial or industrial activity for purposes of combat support or for individual and unit retraining of military personnel or to maintain or strengthen mobilization readiness.

c. A satisfactory commercial source is not available and cannot be developed in time to provide a product or service when it is needed.

d. The product or service is not available from another Federal Agency nor from commercial sources.

e. Procurement of the product or service from a commercial source will result in higher total cost to the Government.[9]

These general rules can be summarized as follows: (1) Uniformed personnel are to be assigned to jobs that, according to the armed forces, require a military incumbent. (2) All other jobs are to be filled by federal civilians or contracted for in the private sector; the services must prove that a military person is required. And (3) reliance on the private sector

7. Department of the Air Force, Air Force Regulation 26-10, "Manpower Utilization," February 24, 1964, p. 2.

8. Office of Management and Budget, "Policies for Acquiring Commercial or Industrial Products and Services for Government Use," Circular no. A-76, revised, October 18, 1976, p. 1.

9. Department of Defense, Directive 4100.15, "Commercial or Industrial Activities," July 8, 1971, p. 3.

is to be encouraged; the service or agency must prove that a "compelling" reason exists to keep certain jobs in-house (within the defense organization).

How are these principles applied? An examination of the decision-making process (a brief description of which is provided in appendix B) reveals that the overall composition of defense manpower is not derived analytically. Manpower issues are raised at several points in the deliberations of the administration and Congress, but usually not in the context of evaluating the relative costs and effectiveness of alternatives for specific activities, and rarely from a "zero base." Even less often is consideration given to possible trade-offs among the several forms of manpower available to the Department of Defense—military, federal civilian, and contract. Such analyses are avoided partly because the process is so complicated (participants seek simple rules, like comparing the current year's request with last year's authorization) and partly because institutional and political forces exert unusual and often conflicting influences. The net tendency is to discourage changes in the manpower mix and to perpetuate the status quo.

Civilian Jobs in the Defense Establishment

Under these guidelines and service regulations civilian employees work in 1,520 different occupations in the Department of Defense, 350 are white-collar jobs and the rest are blue-collar. Table 2-2 shows how the civilians are distributed by occupational group. One-third of them were concentrated in five areas in 1977, working as secretaries, logistics technicians, engineers, mechanics and repairmen, or in general management. Table 2-3 shows how this work force is divided among the categories used by the Pentagon in its fiscal planning: clusters of so-called program elements, each of which includes combinations of resources—people, equipment, installations, and dollars—that make up a military capability or support activity. In these terms, four out of five civilians work in activities whose output is related to supporting combat forces, the majority involved in either logistics (supply and maintenance) or base operations. In fact, civilians constitute close to one-half of all employees in the defense support establishment.

Table 2-2. U.S. Direct Hire Civilian Employees, by Occupational Group, September 1977

Occupational group	Number of employees
Scientists and engineers	
Scientists	14,279
Engineers	55,532
Other professionals	
Mathematicians	5,701
Medical professionals	7,829
Lawyers	1,491
Educators	11,184
Miscellaneous	6,245
Management and administrative personnel	
Logistics managers	49,513
Personnel managers	10,658
Financial managers	21,357
Data systems managers	20,893
Central management employees	71,575
Technicians	
Scientific and engineering technicians	33,652
Medical technicians	4,345
Logistics technicians	58,142
Management technicians	23,856
Miscellaneous technicians	35,773
Clerical workers	
Secretaries	79,689
Financial clerks	16,448
Logistics clerks	9,046
General office operators	29,104
Miscellaneous clerical workers	6,458
Service workers	
Medical attendants	5,483
Firemen and police	18,167
Personnel services employees	24,811
Craftsmen, mechanics, and production workers	
Electronics mechanics	24,193
Electricians	17,878
Machine tool operators	19,021
Metal workers	25,780
Aircraft mechanics	29,119
Pipefitting workers	12,776
Woodworkers	9,419
Marine equipment repairmen	1,125
Miscellaneous mechanics and repairmen	49,613
Miscellaneous production workers	28,945
Laborers and operators	
Vehicle operators	28,883
Logistics workers	41,959
Installation maintenance workers	33,931
Total	943,873

Source: Based on data provided by the Office of the Assistant Secretary of Defense (Manpower, Reserve Affairs, and Logistics), March 1978. Does not include 8,243 employees who were not identified by occupational group.

Table 2-3. Distribution of Defense Civilian Manpower, by Defense Planning and Programming Categories, Fiscal Years 1964 and 1978

Category	Number of civilians (thousands)		Civilians as percentage of total manpower in category		Percentage of total defense civilians	
	1964	1978	1964	1978	1964	1978
Strategic forces	16	13	6.6	11.4	1.4	1.2
General purpose forces	73	78	6.5	7.5	6.2	7.5
Land forces	35	41	5.4	6.9	2.9	4.0
Tactical air forces	8	13	5.2	7.0	0.7	1.3
Naval forces	*	1	*	*	*	*
Mobility forces	31	23	35.7	36.9	2.6	2.2
Auxiliary forces	128	112	42.0	49.0	10.9	10.9
Intelligence and security	12	9	21.9	19.7	1.0	0.9
Communications	14	13	27.1	28.5	1.2	1.3
Research and development	88	76	64.0	71.8	7.4	7.3
Support to other nations	6	4	42.7	43.4	0.5	0.4
Geophysical activities	9	10	35.8	48.8	0.7	1.0
Mission support forces	267	197	34.9	41.5	22.7	19.1
Reserve component support	16	18	35.7	56.8	1.4	1.8
Base operating support	235	168	41.0	46.9	20.0	16.3
Force support training	2	3	3.1	7.6	0.1	0.3
Command	14	8	15.4	17.4	1.2	0.8
Central support forces	692	631	48.8	49.5	58.8	61.2
Base operating support	107	113	65.6	74.4	9.1	11.0
Medical support	32	43	27.8	33.6	2.7	4.2
Personnel support	8	25	26.3	42.8	0.7	2.4
Individual training	30	32	5.9	6.9	2.5	3.1
Command	64	55	57.0	62.9	5.5	5.3
Logistics	483	362	93.2	94.6	38.3	35.2
Total	1,176	1,031	30.6	33.0	100.0	100.0

Sources: Fiscal 1964 figures based on data provided by the Office of the Assistant Secretary of Defense (Program Analysis and Evaluation), January 1977. Fiscal 1978 data are from Office of the Assistant Secretary of Defense (Manpower and Reserve Affairs), "Manpower Requirements Report for FY 1978" (March 1977; processed), p. II-22.

* Less than 500 employees or less than 1 percent.

Cost of Defense Civilian Manpower

Over the past decade, changes in the cost of defense manpower have been among the most important factors shaping the defense budget. Attention for the most part has been directed toward the military side of the ledger. Indeed, the incentives used to ease the transition to an all-volunteer service and the upward trend in military retirement costs have re-

Table 2-4. Projected Defense Civilian Payroll Costs, by Employment Category, Fiscal Year 1978

Category[a]	Average number of employees (thousands)	Total payroll (millions of dollars)
Direct hire		
General schedule	566.6	11,024.9
Wage Board	328.5	6,292.0
Foreign national	36.7	252.0
Indirect hire		
Foreign national	81.0	1,102.7
Total	1,012.8	18,671.6

Source: Based on data provided by the Assistant Secretary of Defense (Comptroller), March 1978.
a. See appendix A for explanation of categories.

ceived wide publicity; but the large costs associated with defense civilians have not.

In its fiscal 1978 budget, the Department of Defense earmarked $18.7 billion to meet its civilian payroll, distributed as shown in table 2-4.[10] This amount, which constitutes about 17 percent of total defense spending and 30 percent of all defense manpower costs, is $8 billion greater than was paid to 375,000 more civilian employees just ten years ago. How the civilian payroll has changed—so that it is 142 percent higher in average per capita pay—is shown in table 2-5.

Rise in White-collar Pay

For white-collar workers, whose average pay more than doubled over the period, the increase can be attributed to two factors: pay equalization and a higher grade structure.

Comparability pay legislation was enacted to bring general schedule salaries up to levels prevailing in the private sector. This was achieved by "catch-up" raises in 1968 and 1969, and subsequent annual increases designed to match those in the private sector.

The average grade of white-collar employees has also increased markedly since 1968, except for a brief period of decline from fiscal 1972 to

10. In addition to direct salaries and wages, the civilian payroll includes the government's contribution to retirement, health insurance, education and training benefits, and the like. To the extent that the civilian retirement system is underfunded, at present rates of contribution, civilian costs, and the defense budget itself, are understated. This issue is discussed in more detail in chapter 5.

Table 2-5. Average Defense Civilian Per Capita Payroll Costs, by Category of Employment, Fiscal Years 1968 and 1978

Amounts in dollars

Category[a]	1968	1978	Percentage increase, 1968–78
Direct hire			
General schedule	9,462	19,458	105.6
Wage Board	8,041	19,154	138.2
Foreign national	1,581	6,866	334.3
Indirect hire			
Foreign national	2,950	13,614	361.5
Total	7,619	18,436	142.0

Source: Based on data provided by the Assistant Secretary of Defense (Comptroller), March 1978.
a. See appendix A for explanation of categories.

1974. One way to measure this growth is to calculate the change in average per capita pay that can be attributed to changes in grade structure. In these terms, growth since 1975 is particularly conspicuous: an average of 1.00 percent a year, in contrast to an average annual growth of 0.63 percent between fiscal 1968 and 1975.

Some analysts contend that the largest part of this increase is due to changes in the occupational mix.[11] While there is evidence that such changes were significant in the late 1960s and early 1970s, it is unlikely that the increase in grade structure experienced since 1975 can be similarly explained. To illustrate the financial dimensions of this phenomenon, consider that if the grade distribution that existed in fiscal 1975 prevailed in fiscal 1978, the 1978 white-collar payroll would be about $350 million lower.

Rise in Blue-collar Wages

For blue-collar workers, the even larger increase over the period, roughly paralleling experience in the private sector, enabled them to maintain a pay advantage that can be attributed largely to the ground rules under which Wage Board pay rates are calculated. Quirks in the

11. According to one Pentagon study, three-fourths of the increase in the average grade of civilians between 1964 and 1976 can be attributed to shifts in the occupational mix. See Walter B. Bergmann and James E. Willoughby, "Analysis of the Causes for the Increasing Trend in DoD General Schedule Average Grade—FY 1964 to FY 1976," Office of the Assistant Secretary of Defense (Manpower and Reserve Affairs) (April 1977; processed).

formula have caused the pay of many of these workers to exceed the levels required to maintain comparability with their counterparts in private industry. This is how it happens.

First, under the present system, pay raises for all federal blue-collar workers are calculated so as to maintain comparability with local prevailing rates in 135 geographically distributed wage areas. Based on surveys of comparable jobs in each area, the law provides that wages paid to workers at step two (of five possible steps in each grade) be pegged to *average* private-sector wages. Pay at step two then becomes the reference point for calculating increases in the remaining steps: government workers in step one receive 96 percent of step two wages, while those in steps three, four, and five receive 104, 108, and 112 percent, respectively. The rub is that four out of five defense blue-collar employees are above step two and the average employee, being close to step four, now receives about 8 percent more than the average private-sector worker in a comparable job. Moreover, over one-half of the government blue-collar force is in pay step five, thus receiving wages about 12 percent above the private-sector average.

Second, under legislation enacted in 1968 (the Monroney amendment),[12] the government is sometimes required to "import" wage rates from one geographical area to another; this results in pay rates for some employees that exceed the local wage level. When the number of private-sector employees in certain specialized jobs is not large enough to provide an adequate basis for survey, private-sector wages for those jobs have to be imported from the nearest appropriate wage area, *providing* that their inclusion will not result in lower federal wages. Moreover, when the imported rates are higher—as they were in 28 of the 135 wage-area surveys in 1976—they actually raise the wages of all federal blue-collar workers in the area, not just those in the specialized occupations for which the data are imported. Thus, according to the Congressional Budget Office, in 1976 about 17 percent of all federal blue-collar employees received increases as much as 25 percent in excess of local private-sector wages.[13]

Finally, federal blue-collar employees who work the night shift are paid a uniform nationwide premium rate; those working the second shift

12. 5 Stat. 5343. See section (d) for details of this ruling. The amendment bears the name of its principal architect, Senator A. S. Mike Monroney, Democrat from Oklahoma.

13. Congressional Budget Office, *The Costs of Defense Manpower: Issues for 1977* (GPO, January 1977), p. 111.

Table 2-6. Comparison of Night Shift Differential Rates for Private-Sector and Federal Employees, Five Selected Areas, 1976

Cents per hour

Location	Private-sector local rate	Federal rate[a]
Los Angeles, California	24	51
Washington, D.C.	27	50
Fort Worth, Texas	18	47
Chicago, Illinois	23	52
Seattle, Washington	30	52

Source: Data provided by the Office of the Assistant Secretary of Defense (Manpower and Reserve Affairs), December 1976.
a. Calculated at a uniform differential of 7.5 percent.

receive a differential of 7.5 percent and those on the third shift receive 10 percent. In a majority of cases, this uniform differential exceeds local rates. How local night-shift rates paid by the private sector differ from those paid by the government is shown in table 2-6. For example, the Pentagon estimates that in the Washington, D.C., area in 1976 the average differential rate for the second shift was about 50 cents an hour for government blue-collar workers, compared with about 27 cents an hour for similar occupations in the local private sector.

Taken together, these anomalies have resulted in pay levels for federal blue-collar workers that, according to the Rockefeller Commission on Federal Compensation, yield "an unfair competitive advantage for the Federal Government, and unjustifiable payroll costs."[14] It is also worth noting that blue-collar workers have escaped the effects of such restraints as the 1975 "pay cap" that have been imposed on the pay of their white-collar and military counterparts.

Administration officials have tried to correct this situation. In 1976, President Ford proposed legislation that would have (1) matched *average* federal wages to *average* local prevailing wages, (2) repealed the Monroney amendment, and (3) replaced the uniform night-shift differential rate with locally established rates. The bill was introduced in the Ninety-fourth Congress but died in committee. Similar legislation was submitted by the Carter administration to the Ninety-fifth Congress, but it was not considered during the first session.

The financial stakes are high. If enacted before October 1978, the proposed measure would yield savings of $136 million in fiscal 1979. Under

14. *Report to the President of the President's Panel on Federal Compensation* (GPO, December 1975), p. 24.

conservative assumptions about future blue-collar pay increases, annual savings would exceed $500 million by 1983, with cumulative savings over the five-year period approaching $2.0 billion, as shown below.[15]

| | *Fiscal years* | | | | | *Cumulative 1979–* |
Reform	*1979*	*1980*	*1981*	*1982*	*1983*	*1983*
Proper matching of average wages	118	318	415	429	451	1,731
Repeal of Monroney amendment	15	36	42	54	57	204
Use of local night-shift differential	3	3	4	5	5	20
Total savings	136	357	461	488	513	1,955

DESPITE its impressive size and the growing demands that it is placing on the Pentagon's budget, the defense civilian work force has attracted little attention. Guidelines governing its use are not followed to the letter. Their vague contours leave a great deal open to interpretation, thus permitting institutional and political forces to exert considerable influence. On the whole, although requirements for military forces are becoming better understood, a detailed rationale for the size and character of the defense civilian work force has thus far remained outside the range of debate.

15. Data provided by the Office of the Assistant Secretary of Defense (Manpower, Reserve Affairs, and Logistics), January 1978.

CHAPTER THREE

SHAPERS OF DEFENSE MANPOWER POLICY: BUREAUCRATS AND POLITICIANS

Changes over the past twenty-five years—in technology, in support infrastructure, in overseas deployment, and in military organizations—would seem to call for alterations, on technical grounds alone, in the mix of civilians and uniformed personnel. Yet the stability of the civilian percentage suggests that factors not strictly related to national security may influence the composition of the defense work force. Bureaucrats and political leaders, who are the *real* shapers of defense manpower policy, have many other considerations to take into account.

Bureaucratic Interests

The imprecise and vague guidelines provided by the Office of Management and Budget and the secretary of defense give the military services wide latitude in determining the composition of their work forces. Military managers—and it is they who make most key manpower decisions—tend to prefer uniformed rather than civilian employees. They consider that with uniformed personnel they have greater control over the work force, that a man in uniform projects a stronger signal of U.S. military commitment abroad, and that uniformed employees are less subject to reductions in force and cost less.

Management Flexibility

The most common rationale for the military's preference for uniformed rather than civilian personnel is greater flexibility in the management of military employees. Among the limitations on the control of civilian workers perceived by military managers are the following:

1. Restrictions on authority to transfer or reassign civilian employees at management's discretion.

15

2. Problems in dealing effectively with the marginal employee.

3. Restraints [imposed by provisions] of the civilian employee retirement system.

4. Restraints on effective management of the workforce during reductions in force (RIF).

5. Lack of mobility of the civilian workforce.

6. Restrictions and controls on management of the work week for the civilian workforce.[1]

The extent to which these perceptions are valid is the subject of some controversy. For example, the discretionary authority of a military commander to issue a rifle to and press into combat duty, say, a behind-the-lines supply clerk has long epitomized the flexibility argument. However, the merits of viewing all military personnel, regardless of training and skill, as potentially available for combat are less persuasive now than they were in the past. In contrast to an earlier era in which foot-slogging riflemen constituted the principal combat element, the highly specialized nature of modern warfare requires personnel trained to operate sophisticated weaponry. Support personnel would probably have to undergo intensive training to become effective in modern combat units.

Similarly, the extent to which the other factors mentioned by military managers actually limit effective control over civilian employees is an open question, discussed further in chapter 7. What is important, however, is that such constraints are perceived by these planners and managers as immutable. One reason for this attitude is the sharp difference between the military and civilian personnel systems.

The military system can be characterized as "closed," person-oriented, and centralized, while the system governing the management of civilians is "open," job-oriented, and decentralized. Military people usually enter at the bottom of the grade structure; they are trained and then, as they progress through the system in a sequence of career-broadening assignments, achieve appropriate rank and pay raises.

Civilians, on the other hand, move in and out of the civil service, with grade and pay vested in the job rather than the individual. Partly because of these features, the military personnel system receives more attention; long-range centralized planning is necessary to ensure that people with the right skills and experience are available when they are needed. Since

1. Howard W. Goheen, "Limitations on Managers Brought About by Restrictions of the Federal Civil Service System," in Defense Manpower Commission, *Defense Manpower Commission Staff Studies,* vol. 4 (Government Printing Office, 1976), p. 3.

trained civilians can be hired and enter the system in any job at any level, long-term planning that includes training programs and career-broadening assignments is not considered as important. For these reasons, the management of civilian personnel is generally left to the local base commanders or facility managers, who have the responsibility to create, abolish, classify, and fill civilian positions. Because of this decentralization, policies and regulations governing civil service employees are interpreted locally and often erroneously.

Military Personnel and Foreign Policy

Another less controversial rationale put forward is the advantage of employing military rather than civilian personnel in fulfilling U.S. foreign policy objectives. The importance of the defense manpower mix on the image projected abroad cannot be discounted. According to some defense planners, military establishments are judged in the international arena as much by aggregate symbols (defense budget as a percentage of gross national product; number of divisions, air wings, and ships; and total number of men *in uniform*) as they are by more abstract measures of military capability. And there is little doubt that foreign leaders—allies and adversaries alike—are influenced more by the size of military forces (2 million) than by the size of the total defense establishment (3 million, including civilians). For, after all, military manpower is associated with combat and the civilian work force with support. The military—whatever their duties—are perceived as symbols of American commitment and resolve.

Even more important, some argue, are the foreign policy signals that accompany *changes* in the size of the uniformed force. Foreign leaders, it is contended, are likely to associate a large reduction in military manpower with a diminution in willingness to fulfill foreign commitments. Indeed, some would hold that even small reductions could have this effect if a level with symbolic significance, such as a military force "two million strong" went by the board.

Vulnerability of Civilian Strength

Many Pentagon decisionmakers apparently consider that civilian employees are more vulnerable than the military to reductions in force. This concern is not without foundation; according to the House Armed Services Committee:

Civilian manpower, by its very nature, is in a support role, and is an element that should receive first consideration when reductions are taken.[2]

Also still fresh in the minds of defense planners are the circumstances surrounding the last major civilian substitution. In 1973 the program to replace 48,000 military with 40,000 civilians was undertaken in part to reduce the requirement for military manpower and thus to stave off the recruitment problems expected to accompany the transition to an all-volunteer force. Congress followed in fiscal 1975 and 1976, however, by proposing a sharp reduction—some 55,000—in civilian personnel. In the face of growing uncertainty about the ability to maintain a military force of 2 million at present standards of "quality" by voluntary means, pressures for further substitution have intensified.

Higher Cost of Civilian Manpower

Many military managers subscribe to the thesis that civilian employees are not only less effective than their military counterparts but also more costly. Whether or not this is the case, their conclusions seem to be based more on intuition than on analysis. Misconceptions may arise because relative costs (discussed in chapter 5) are hard to assess. In the first place, striking differences in military and civilian pay systems make valid comparisons difficult, so that, in the absence of accepted standards, military personnel often compare civilian salaries (the bulk of the civilian compensation package) with military basic pay, which constitutes from only 50 to 75 percent of total military compensation. And, second, there are no accepted rules for establishing equivalent military and civilian grades. Moreover, some military officials are undoubtedly influenced by their memories of the underpaid military conscript who no longer exists. But, with the advent of comparability standards and the transition to the all-volunteer force, military pay, particularly at the lower levels, has been increased substantially.

2. *Authorizing Appropriations, Fiscal Year 1976 and the Period Beginning July 1, 1976, and Ending September 30, 1976, for Military Procurement, Research and Development; Strengths for Active-Duty Military Components; Reserve Components and Civilian Personnel of the Defense Establishment; Military Training Student Loads; and for Other Purposes,* H. Rept. 199, 94:1 (GPO, 1975), p. 74.

Domestic Politics

Manpower issues are particularly vulnerable to domestic politics. Indeed, Congress is ambivalent about changes in the size or composition of the defense work force. Both liberals and conservatives have shown concern for the growing cost of defense manpower—the former because of the drain it imposes on federal spending and the latter because it leaves the Pentagon with too little to invest in weapons. With few exceptions, members of both groups appear to favor a reduction in defense manpower costs, preferably on the civilian side since reductions there are seen as lesser risks to national security.[3] They, like the White House, attempt to exert pressure through the imposition of ceilings.

Yet both groups are also subject—and succumb most often—to the countervailing pressures exerted by their constituencies, especially when civilian reductions are under discussion, since their local communities and special interest groups are affected.

Local Economic Effects

Civilians are predominantly in supporting activities so that proposed reductions in civilian manpower are often linked with the consolidation or closing of facilities, whereas those in the military generally affect many geographically dispersed units. Civilian reductions therefore have a more direct and noticeable economic impact on a community.

The political implications of defense employment are vividly illustrated by the attempts made by the New England Congressional Caucus in 1977 to stave off reductions at Loring Air Force Base in Maine. Pointing out

3. To illustrate the unusual coalitions that form around such issues, Senators William Proxmire and Barry Goldwater in 1975 cosponsored an amendment to reduce defense civilian end strength to a figure 17,000 below that proposed by the Senate Armed Services Committee. Despite opposition from Senators John C. Stennis and Sam Nunn, both of whom favored more gradual reductions, the amendment passed 42–40. It is often possible for two powerful legislators who normally disagree to marshall unexpected support, when they agree. For example, Senator Robert Dole, a devotee of a strong defense, voted for the amendment. It is indicative of the unpredictability of the issue, however, that Senators Walter F. Mondale and Hubert H. Humphrey voted against it. See *Congressional Record,* vol. 121, pt. 13, 94:1 (GPO, 1975), pp. 17089–95.

that "equal sacrifices should be made by all regions when defense personnel cutbacks must be made," a study by the caucus showed that New England lost about 51 percent of its defense employment between 1960 and 1975, while the United States as a whole experienced a decrease of less than 10 percent.[4] Moreover, it has been reported that the Northeast-Midwest Economic Advancement Coalition has begun an all-out effort to swing defense spending from the southern and western states which, according to the coalition, now enjoy a disproportionate share of the Pentagon's budget.[5]

It did not take long for the White House to indicate some sensitivity to such political pressures. Two recent issues are the relocation of the Second Infantry Division and the modernization of the aircraft carrier, *Saratoga.* The Carter administration is reportedly leaning toward relocating the Second Infantry Division, scheduled for withdrawal from South Korea, to three bases in the Northeast: Fort Drum, New York; Fort Dix, New Jersey; and Fort Devens, Massachusetts. Army officials, on the other hand, concerned about the adverse cost-and-effectiveness implications of splitting up the division, are reported to prefer Fort Bliss, Texas, or Fort Benning, Georgia. In the case of the *Saratoga,* the Navy selected the government-owned yard at Philadelphia as the site for the ship's overhaul, despite reports that it would cost $30 million less at the privately owned Newport News, Virginia, shipyard. Coincident with the Navy's announcement was Vice President Mondale's statement: "I am pleased to announce that our efforts to alleviate the adverse effect of the closing of the Frankford Arsenal [Philadelphia] have now been successful." However, prompted by two Virginia legislators, the fiscal year 1979 defense authorization bill was amended to prevent the assignment of the overhaul to any location, pending completion of a Navy study of the comparative costs at private and public shipyards.[6]

Although many factors are involved in these two complicated issues, the important influence of domestic politics cannot be denied.

4. New England Congressional Caucus, News Release, August 9, 1977.

5. Reported in *Chicago Tribune,* August 30, 1977.

6. For accounts of the Second Infantry Division issue, see *New York Times,* January 5, 1978, and *Army Times,* April 24, 1978. For accounts of the *Saratoga* issue, see *New York Times,* June 11, 1978, and Vice President Walter F. Mondale's statement in connection with the U.S. Navy's announcement that the aircraft carrier U.S.S. *Saratoga* was to be sent to Philadelphia for modernization in late 1980, News Release, April 14, 1978.

Ceiling Controls

Both Congress and the White House exert influence on the defense civilian work force principally through the imposition of ceilings. Their most common rationale is that ceilings encourage efficiency, but they serve two other purposes as well.

CEILINGS TO BRAKE BUREAUCRATIC GROWTH. The first has been succinctly stated:

The Congress, the President, and OMB are concerned about effective, efficient, and economical use of manpower, but they lack assurance that the agencies would effectively control employment levels if they were not constrained by numerical ceilings.[7]

In other words, policymakers apparently feel that restrictions on funding levels are not sufficient to restrain the growth of the federal bureaucracy. This argument presumes that defense planners are clamoring to increase the size of the civilian component of their labor force, a presumption that flies in the face of experience, at least in the Department of Defense. Unlike other government agencies, counterpressures exist in the Pentagon; civilian personnel are not the essence of the defense organization. The natural predilection toward filling jobs with uniformed employees, on the one hand, and the unusually heavy financial demands of capital equipment, on the other, are sufficient checks on growth. Indeed, it could be argued that some form of external pressure (such as the imposition of civilian substitution programs) is needed before additional jobs are opened to federal civilian employees, even when it can be demonstrated that they cost less than military personnel.

CEILINGS AS A POLITICAL INSTRUMENT. The most recent evidence of personnel ceilings being used as a political instrument is the reduction in the number of federal employees imposed in June 1977 by the Carter administration. On the surface, this arbitrary reduction in the federal civilian work force, presumably to be accomplished by normal attrition and unrelated to workload, appeared to be simply a gesture toward fulfillment of a campaign pledge to streamline the federal bureaucracy.

If experience is a reliable guide, this will result in a less-than-orderly conduct of business in fiscal 1978 and 1979. The most common adjust-

7. Comptroller General of the United States, *Personnel Ceilings—A Barrier to Effective Manpower Management* (General Accounting Office, 1977), p. 72.

ment will be to attempt to sustain the activity at the approved budget level by using outside contractors. Because of the limitations imposed on contracting by Congress in 1977, discussed below, the use of private enterprise is somewhat circumscribed, but is still possible. In other cases, temporary civil servants may be cut near the end of the fiscal year and additional workers may be put on overtime. With the additional constraint that no full-time workers are to be terminated, the Department of Defense will have to relocate personnel from activities that are cut to other activities, in some cases even when skills do not match job requirements.

Government Competition with Private Enterprise

Successive administrations over the past twenty-five years or so have altered the ground rules for decisions about whether government or the private sector should conduct quasi-commercial activities. Politics have certainly been in evidence in discussions of policies governing the mix of defense employees and contract labor.

THE EISENHOWER ADMINISTRATION. For example, to offset what he perceived as a disturbing trend of government competition with private enterprise over the twenty years of the Roosevelt and Truman administrations, President Dwight D. Eisenhower stated in 1954:

This budget [for fiscal 1955] marks the beginning of a movement to shift . . . to private enterprise, Federal activities which can be more appropriately and more efficiently carried on in that way.[8]

The thrust of this message was later reflected in executive policy through a series of Bureau of the Budget bulletins, which clearly based the policy of government procurement from commercial sources on the desirability of supporting the free enterprise system:

Because the private enterprise system is basic to the American economy, the general policy establishes a presumption in favor of Government procurement from commercial sources. This has the two-fold benefit of furthering the free enterprise system and permitting agencies to concentrate their efforts on their primary objectives.[9]

THE KENNEDY-JOHNSON ERA. With the change in administration in 1961, a number of studies were made to examine the implications of this

8. "Annual Budget Message to the Congress: Fiscal Year 1955, January 21, 1954," *Public Papers of the Presidents, Dwight D. Eisenhower, 1954* (GPO, 1960), p. 81.
9. Bureau of the Budget, Bulletin no. 60-2, September 21, 1959.

policy. One, completed by the Department of Defense in 1965, concluded that, while some contracts with the private sector were in conflict with civil service laws and were also more costly than similar work done by defense employees, many support services were being done in-house, "which, on the basis of realistic cost comparisons, might better be accomplished by the use of contractor support."[10] On March 3, 1966, the Bureau of the Budget bulletin quoted above was canceled and replaced by an Office of Management and Budget circular, which made a number of changes in policies and procedures. The new circular did not explicitly overturn the government's general policy of relying on the private enterprise system, but it limited reliance on private contractors to an extent consistent with effective and efficient accomplishment of government programs.

THE NIXON-FORD YEARS. Although no major alterations in policy were forthcoming during the Nixon-Ford administration, two changes made in 1976 clearly moved government agencies back toward greater reliance on private enterprise. The 1966 circular was changed in October 1976 so as to require computations that made operations by federal civilians more costly in relation to contract operations. The most significant change increased the cost of retirement from 7 percent to 24.7 percent of basic pay.[11] In a separate action, each department and agency was expected to identify "at least five functions presently performed in-house" that could be reviewed for possible transfer to the private sector.[12]

THE CARTER ADMINISTRATION. Barely four months into his administration, President Jimmy Carter announced plans to take a fresh look into the issue. Pending completion of a review, the retirement cost factor to be used was reduced from 24.7 to 14.1 percent and the "five-function" quota approach established by the Ford administration was discontinued.[13] The results of the review were made public in November 1977 when the administration proposed a series of policy changes. Besides clarifying basic principles and definitions, the administration's proposal

10. Department of Defense, "Contract Support Services Project Staff Report" (March 1965; processed), p. 8.

11. Office of Management and Budget, "Policies of Acquiring Commercial or Industrial Products and Services for Government Use," Circular no. A-76, revised, October 18, 1976, p. 2.

12. Office of Management and Budget, "Presidential Management Initiatives," Memorandum to Cabinet Members and Heads of Major Agencies, July 27, 1976.

13. Office of Management and Budget, "Director's Talking Paper," Press conference, OMB Circular A-76, June 13, 1977.

advocates a civil service retirement cost factor of 20.4 percent of salary, a figure that is to be subject to periodic review. Also, analyses comparing the cost of conducting an existing in-house activity to the cost of contracting for the activity are to use a differential of 10 percent of personnel costs favoring continuation in-house. On the other hand, analyses comparing the cost of a proposed new in-house activity to the cost of contracting are to use a differential of 10 percent of the estimated personnel costs and 25 percent of the estimated facilities and matériel costs favoring the contracting option. The net effect of this compromise is to give private industry an advantage in bidding for new jobs while at the same time protecting jobs that are now performed by federal civilians.[14]

Special Interests

Special interest groups, such as the American Federation of Government Employees (AFGE), are a force to be reckoned with in civilian manpower planning. This union is very active on Capitol Hill and can be expected to work against any reductions in federal civilian manpower. Its influence is felt, for example, in the current congressional concern over the contract labor issue. By most accounts, federal blue-collar workers are paid at rates higher on average than their private-sector counterparts, as a consequence of anomalies in the formula for calculating annual pay increases (chapter 2). On a cost-effectiveness basis, therefore, procurement of services by private contract would appear to be more attractive than having the work done in-house by blue-collar civilians. Nonetheless, the AFGE lobbied strongly and successfully to forestall a proposal by the Ford administration that would have changed the blue-collar pay formula and made in-house programs more competitive, and the organization is working to ward off similar attempts by the Carter administration to alter the blue-collar pay system.

Meanwhile, the AFGE has also lobbied intensively to prevent increases in the amount of work contracted out. In testimony before the Senate Armed Services Subcommittee on Manpower and Personnel, AFGE President Kenneth T. Blaylock claimed that it was rarely cheaper for government agencies to turn jobs over to private industry. Even when it appears to reduce costs, according to Blaylock, reliance on the private sector may lead to "loss of government capability or control over the

14. *Federal Register,* November 21, 1977, pp. 59814–26.

function, loss of government accountability, defaults of contractors, poor performance by contractors . . . etc."[15] In warning that contractors are going to underbid in-house proposals, Subcommittee Chairman Senator Sam Nunn indicated the dilemma posed by the situation: "The issue is almost one of wage levels versus jobs. . . . I don't see how you can have it both ways."[16]

As matters turned out, the union came close to having it both ways, at least temporarily. Although Congress did make small cuts in civilian manpower, the fiscal 1978 defense appropriation bill prohibits contracting out of a wide variety of base operating support activities now performed by government employees. Taking a somewhat more liberal stance on weapon system engineering and logistics support, intermediate and depot level maintenance, and research and development, Congress permits the private contract option as long as the work involved is not on a military base or does not cause a reduction in federal employees.[17] The influence of union lobbying on this legislation is hard to assess, but by most accounts it was great.

There are also a number of associations lobbying on behalf of private interests. Among the most active is the National Council of Technical Service Industries. Representing such organizations as Hughes Aircraft Company, Lockheed Aircraft Corporation, and Boeing Services International, NCTSI is dedicated to the idea that free enterprise can best supply most of the support services needed for efficient government operations.

THE SIZE and character of the defense civilian work force are determined not only by technical requirements, but also by institutional interests and domestic politics. Indeed, many factors largely unrelated to national security play an important role in shaping the defense work force. Military planners, usually backed by their civilian leaders, are inclined to protect uniformed personnel. And while many legislators are concerned about the high cost of defense manpower, particularly on the civilian side, they are often torn between national security interests and the particular desires of local constituencies and special interest groups. On balance, these and other conflicting interests discourage more than marginal changes and tend to perpetuate the status quo.

15. Quoted in *Federal Times,* July 25, 1977.
16. Quoted in ibid.
17. *Department of Defense Appropriation Authorization Act, 1978,* S. Rept. 282, 95:1 (GPO, 1977), pp. 14–15.

CHAPTER FOUR

EFFICIENCIES IN THE USE OF CIVILIAN MANPOWER

The continuing debate on the appropriate size of the U.S. defense establishment was intensified by the drawdown in U.S. forces involved in Southeast Asia. As force levels (Army divisions, Navy ships, and Air Force wings) declined after hostilities ended in Vietnam, defense manpower did not decline proportionately. Attracting the largest share of attention was the defense support establishment—and for good reason. The total number of personnel used to man, train, direct, and sustain each combat unit was on the rise. In 1974, the Pentagon unveiled plans to increase manpower efficiency, calling for improvements in the "tooth-to-tail," or combat-to-support manpower, relationships. Three additional Army divisions were to be formed and four Air Force fighter wings filled out by reducing the number of support personnel. Table 4-1 shows that between fiscal 1975 and 1978 combat manpower increased by 4 percent whereas manpower in noncombat units decreased by 7 percent. Most of the reductions in noncombat units were uniformed personnel.

While further efficiencies in the utilization of military manpower are possible and should be sought, this discussion concentrates on the civilian component—mainly on base operations and logistics functions, which together account for the employment of two-thirds of all civilians.

Base Operations Support

The defense base structure consists of 5,822 separate installations and properties covering close to 28 million acres of land (an area larger than the state of Tennessee) with an original real property investment cost estimated at more than $44 billion.[1] Counting active duty, reserve, retired, dependent, and civilian personnel, these bases serve over 10 million people. All together, about one-half million people (of which 45 percent are military) operate these installations and provide a wide range of services: buildings and grounds maintenance, supply, transportation, utilities, equipment maintenance, communications, administrative services, security, fire protection, commissaries, churches, and the like. In many respects base operating support personnel provide services similar to those provided by local governments, utilities, and the service industry segment of the civilian economy.

The number of installations operated by each military department and the number of personnel involved in operating those installations are as follows:[2]

	Installations		*Number of base operations personnel (thousands)*		
Component	*Number*	*Area (millions of acres)*	*Military*	*Civilian*	*Total*
Army	2,293	12.7	45.4	126.6	172.0
Navy and Marine Corps	764	4.3	54.1	63.7	117.8
Air Force	2,765	10.9	128.9	84.6	213.5
Defense agencies	. . .	. . .	. . .	5.9	5.9
Total	5,882	27.8	228.4	280.8	509.2

What is the justification for this base structure and the sizable allocation of manpower (about one-sixth of the defense work force) to operate it? The links between a given combat force, its basing requirements, and the cost of operating its bases have not been well established. The Department of Defense issues the following rationales:

The size of the base structure is dependent upon many factors such as the number of active peacetime authorized military and civilian personnel; the peacetime forces approved for these manpower levels; force deployments over-

1. Office of the Assistant Secretary of Defense (Installations and Logistics), "Base Structure Annex to Manpower Requirements Report for FY 1978" (February 1977; processed), p. 7. An obvious definitional problem arises in any discussion of the defense base structure. The distinctions between installations, properties, and bases, for example, are not sharp. A Navy "base complex," like Norfolk, may be counted as thirty installations, while all comparable functions might be found on a single Army base.

2. Ibid., pp. 8, 9; and Office of the Assistant Secretary of Defense (Manpower and Reserve Affairs), "Manpower Requirements for FY 1978" (March 1977; processed), pp. II-23–26, II-33–37.

Table 4-1. Trends in Defense Manpower, Fiscal Years 1975 and 1978

Manpower in thousands

Manpower category	1975 Military	1975 Civilian	1975 Total	1978 Military	1978 Civilian	1978 Total	Percentage change Military	Percentage change Civilian	Percentage change Total
Combat	1,009.7	90.7	1,100.4	1,050.3	90.6	1,140.9	+4	…	+4
Strategic	111.2	10.6	121.8	100.7	12.8	113.5	−9	+21	−7
General purpose	898.5	80.1	978.6	949.6	77.8	1,027.4	+6	−3	+5
Noncombat	801.7	987.6	1,789.3	717.8	940.2	1,658.0	−10	−5	−7
Auxiliary forces[a]	137.7	121.3	259.0	119.1	112.0	231.1	−14	−8	−11
Support forces[b]	664.0	866.3	1,530.3	598.7	828.2	1,426.9	−10	−4	−7
Individuals[c]	315.9	…	315.9	320.9	…	320.9	+2	…	+2
Total	2,127.3	1,078.4	3,205.7	2,089.0	1,030.7	3,119.7	−2	−4	−3

Source: Fiscal 1975 data, Department of Defense, "Manpower Requirements Report for FY 1977" (February 1976; processed), pp. II-18, II-20; fiscal 1978 data, Office of the Assistant Secretary of Defense (Manpower and Reserve Affairs), "Manpower Requirements Report for FY 1978" (March 1977; processed), pp. II-20, II-22.

a. Auxiliary forces include personnel involved in intelligence, communications, research and development, support to other nations, and geophysical activities.

b. Support forces include personnel providing base operating support, training, command, medical and personnel support, reserve component support, logistics, and support to other federal agencies.

c. Includes students, transients, patients, prisoners, and cadets.

seas which are required to meet U.S. commitments; the approved Reserve Component force levels; the projected peacetime accession rates for trainees; weapons technology; training methods; tactics; real property investment at existing bases; and contingency and mobilization requirements. In addition to these general factors, each of the force categories such as strategic forces, tactical air forces, airlift forces, etc., has special needs related to dispersion, air defense, redundancy, geography, weather, terrain, and other considerations which greatly affect the base structure.

Each of the four Military Services also has unique requirements which influence the size and composition of its base structure. For the Army, bases must encompass large land areas in order to carry out required training and maneuvers. In general, the Air Force requires appropriately dispersed air bases with good flying weather, adequate and sufficient air space and proximity to training ranges for the most efficient peacetime training operations. The Navy must be located in properly dispersed shore complexes with ready access to deep water and the oceans. The Navy's airfields, therefore, should be clustered as close as possible to its primary port complexes. The Marine Corps, because of its amphibious landing missions, must also be generally situated along the shore with sufficient land area available to carry out the required training.[3]

To go beyond that generalization, to rationalize more specifically the requirements for the numbers, kind, size, and location of military bases, is a difficult task. And, given the many highly emotional nontechnical factors that make even small changes in the base structure difficult, the military services have little incentive to develop the models and techniques necessary to analyze their basing needs. Nor has the job been tackled outside the Pentagon; neither the data nor the methods are available to do so.[4]

Closure and Consolidation

Any estimates of potential savings that would result from eliminating marginal installations are highly speculative. In the early 1970s, Deputy Secretary of Defense David Packard, on leaving his Pentagon post, indicated that about $1 billion a year could be saved if bases could be closed without regard to nonmilitary factors.[5] Since then, some bases have been closed but there is apparently room for further savings.

3. "Base Structure Annex to Manpower Requirements Report for FY 1978," pp. 5–6.

4. Apparently work has started on one piece of the puzzle. The Department of Defense Material Distribution System Study Group, under the auspices of the joint logistics commanders, has recently set about rationalizing the defense supply network. No results were available by time of publication, however.

5. Reported in *Washington Post,* December 14, 1971.

The sprawling Navy shore establishment has come under particular fire. In 1973, the chief of naval operations testified that "the shore establishment was so large in comparison to the dwindling Navy that . . . it was immoral not to make some dramatic reductions in the short establishment."[6] Yet little has since been done.

More recently, a senior Air Force official exposed excesses in the Air Force base structure. In 1976, General Paul K. Carlton, commander of the Military Airlift Command, stated: "I operate about 20 percent more bases than I need to," a situation that, he suggested, "goes all the way through the Department of Defense."[7]

In April 1978 the Carter administration announced its intention "to realign, reduce or close 85 military installations and activities in the U.S."[8] Full implementation of this proposal would eliminate about 14,600 military and 8,600 civilian positions—a modest achievement in light of earlier estimates.

If the base structure could be streamlined, what could be saved? Much would depend on assumptions concerning the proportion of manpower providing base services that would not necessarily vary with changes in the number of installations: those related to maintaining the base itself (for example, road repairs and power generation) that could be reduced only if the base were closed. Those required by people who are dependent on the base (for example, food services and transportation) would vary, of course, with the base population. The larger the proportion of these variable services on any given base, the less would be the savings associated with closing that base. If a base is closed, but the missions associated with it are relocated rather than discontinued, additional personnel might have to be provided at other installations. Net manpower savings would depend on whether the latter bases had excess capacity to absorb additional missions without increasing support personnel. By and large, it is concluded that, unless missions are eliminated, savings would be largely confined to the first, or fixed, base operating service component.

According to the Department of Defense, about 37 percent of total

6. Testimony of Admiral Elmo R. Zumwalt, Jr., *Base Closures or Realignment Program, California,* Hearings before the Subcommittee on Military Construction of the Senate Armed Services Committee, 93:1 (Government Printing Office, 1973) pt. 3, p. 136.

7. Quoted in *Houston Post,* November 28, 1976.

8. Office of the Assistant Secretary of Defense (Public Affairs), "Secretary of Defense Announces New Base Realignment Proposals," News Release no. 214-78, April 26, 1978.

base operations manpower are "fixed."[9] The proportion of 25 percent is assumed in an independent analysis by the staff members of the Defense Manpower Commission.[10] Other studies indicate larger amounts. For example, an analysis of Navy complexes found that the fixed percentage of base operations manpower assigned to naval and fleet air stations ranged from 40 to 60 percent, and reached as high as 90 percent for certain training installations.[11]

Thus the issue is far from settled. But, in the face of this wide variation and in the absence of better information on the precise relationship between base operations support and mission populations, it seems reasonable to assume that fixed and variable base operations support manpower are split evenly. Under that assumption a 20 percent reduction in the number of military installations of average size would yield manpower savings of about 50,000, of which about 27,500 would be civilian (assuming that the proportion of civilian manpower in the fixed component was the same as that in total base operations manpower), provided, of course, that sufficient excess capacity existed in the remaining bases to absorb the mission-related personnel who would be displaced.

This is just a rough approximation. Since the underlying assumption is that the number of people required in the variable support component is directly related to the size of the mission forces, the estimate may be too low. Additional savings may accrue because of economies of scale as units are consolidated, but these are believed to be small.

Of course, if installations with a large fixed support component were selected for reduction, manpower savings would be larger. In the absence of adequate data to measure the fixed-cost component of different installations, a rough indication is the ratio of the number of people being served to the number providing services. For example, in table 4-2, among Air Force bases supporting the strategic air mission, Blytheville Air Force Base, Arkansas, and Wurtsmith Air Force Base, Michigan, both with relatively low mission to base support population ratios stand out.

9. Department of Defense, "Military Manpower Requirements for FY 1973" (February 1972; processed), p. 79.

10. Marvin N. Gordon and John D. Sitterson, Jr., "The Support Forces," in *Defense Manpower Commission, Defense Manpower Commission Staff Studies,* vol. 2 (GPO, 1976), p. 126.

11. Kenneth A. Goudreau, Richard A. Kuzmack, and Karen Weidemann, "Analysis of Closure Alternatives for Naval Stations and Naval Air Stations," Center for Naval Analyses Professional Paper no. 135 (June 1975; processed), pp. 36–38.

Table 4-2. Base Operations Support and Mission Manpower, Selected Air Force Bases with Strategic Air Mission, June 1975

Air force base	Base operations support population	Mission population	Ratio of mission to base operations support populations
Blytheville, Arkansas	1,350	1,730	1.28
Beale, California	1,930	3,635	1.88
March, California	2,060	3,569	1.73
Loring, Maine	1,830	2,850	1.56
Wurtsmith, Michigan	1,525	1,815	1.19
Griffiss, New York	2,300	5,146	2.23
Dyess, Texas	1,740	3,625	2.08

Source: Office of the Assistant Secretary of Defense (Installations and Logistics), "Preliminary Report to the Senate Appropriations Committee on Domestic Base Factors" (March 1977; processed), pp. 29–30.

All in all, the evidence suggests that rather dramatic changes in base structure might result in only modest changes in civilian manpower.

Improving Base Efficiency

Potentially larger, and certainly more politically feasible, are savings that might result from altering the variable component of base operating support. Military planners believe that each installation is unique and they would argue that broad generalizations should not be made. Yet, to meet budget constraints in the past, Pentagon planners have adjusted aggregate rates of variable support.

There are also data indicating that the amount of variable support currently provided may be higher than necessary. Comparison of the operations at Vance Air Force Base and Reese Air Force Base, discussed in chapter 6, indicates that Vance (operated by private contractors) accomplishes essentially the same mission as Reese (operated by in-house personnel) with 71 percent of the manpower and 85 percent of the budget. About two-thirds of the difference was attributed to the management approach used by the contractor:

He [the contractor] employed about one third of the number of supervisors that the Air Force used and the aggregation of his management approaches indicated that he was more concerned with accomplishing the task than organizing to meet a management structure.[12]

12. Robert M. Paulson and Arnold Zimmer, *An Analysis of Methods of Base Support: Contractor Operations versus Standard Operations at Two Undergraduate Pilot Training Bases* (Rand Corporation, March 1975), p. vi.

Other Air Force in-house and contract bids also indicate that in-house operations are more labor-intensive than necessary. In the competition for major nonmilitary support functions at some thirteen aircraft control and warning squadrons in Alaska, for example, the Air Force's in-house bid for the job was close to $100 million higher than that of RCA, the private-sector winner.[13] The consistency with which in-house bids exceed contract bids is evident in a study disclosing that between fiscal 1973 and fiscal 1975, seventy out of seventy-nine comparisons made by the Air Force favored contractors.[14] Such results suggest that either the Air Force is using arbitrarily high manning factors or government operations are inherently more costly because of bureaucratic layering, the inflexible use of manpower, and the like.[15] In either case, it follows that adoption of private enterprise management and manning criteria could lead to savings in manpower.

The Logistics Establishment

Logistics programs include centrally managed supply, maintenance, and support activities that: (1) procure equipment and supplies; (2) store matériel and control inventories; (3) manage and perform depot maintenance; (4) provide printing, laundry, and public works services; and (5) maintain reserve ships and aircraft for use in case of national emergencies. About 383,000 defense employees, the bulk of which are civilians, are involved in these activities, as shown below (in thousands):[16]

Logistics function	Military employees	Civilian employees	Total employees
Supply	6.7	115.0	121.7
Maintenance	8.6	212.5	221.1
Other support	5.2	34.7	39.9
Total	20.5	362.3	382.8

13. "Statement of Ronald V. Paolucci on behalf of Aerospace Industries Association of America, Inc., and Others before the Subcommittee on Manpower and Personnel," Senate Armed Services Committee (July 12, 1977; processed), p. 5.

14. Norman E. Betaque, Jr., and Thomas M. O'Hern, Jr., "Contracting for Services in the Department of Defense," in Defense Manpower Commission, *Defense Manpower Commission Staff Studies*, vol. 2 (GPO, 1976), p. 24.

15. Skeptics might suggest that these results may also be a consequence of "buy in" tactics; that is, underbidding by contractors attempting to get a foot in the door.

16. "Manpower Requirements Report for FY 1978," p. VIII-18.

The debate over the appropriate size of the defense logistics establishment and the efficiency with which it operates has intensified recently because of concern over the state of readiness of U.S. forces. Some observers argue that the military services tend to allocate an inordinate share of their limited resources to the procurement of new weapon systems at the expense of operating and maintaining the ones they already own.[17] But some critics contend that the absence of appropriate "criteria of sufficiency" relating logistic support to the readiness of operational forces has permitted the logistics establishment to assume a life of its own independent of national security requirements. The former would hold that decreases in the size of the defense logistics base could risk national security unduly; the latter, critical of the bureaucratic inertia that makes changes, particularly in a downward direction, difficult, would argue that substantial economies are possible. In truth, both positions are highly speculative and will remain so until better data and better tools of analysis become available.

An evaluation of the quality of current data available for resource allocation decisions on ship maintenance, made by the Department of the Navy in 1977, gives an indication of how much needs to be done to improve data gathering. The following is a summary of the findings:[18]

Resource category	Resource data	Output indicators	Feedback data
Supply of repair parts	Good	Fair	Sketchy
Manpower	Fragmented	Fair	Fair
Technical documentation	Fair	Fragmented	None
Test equipment	Available but misused	None	None
On-site technical assistance	None	None	None
Product improvement	Fragmented	None	None
Other fleet modernization	Fair to poor	None	None
Intermediate maintenance	Good	Inadequate	Fair
Depot maintenance	Good	Fragmented	Good on resources but none on impact

17. See, for example, the results of an analysis by Senator John Culver, *Congressional Record,* daily ed., April 6, 1977, pp. S5696–99.

18. Department of the Navy, "Program Objective Memorandum, FY 1979–1983 (POM-79)" (1977; processed), Annex D, p. 4.

Table 4-3. Ship Overhaul Costs, Selected Fiscal Years 1968–78

Item	1968	1973	1978	Percentage change 1968–78
Number of ship overhauls	230	82	77	−67
Ship overhaul cost (millions of current dollars)	396.7	498.6	1,555.2	292
Ship overhaul cost (millions of 1978 dollars)[a]	820.4	774.3	1,555.2	90
Cost per overhaul (millions of 1978 dollars)[a]	3.57	9.44	20.2	466

Source: Office of the Chief of Naval Operations, "Historical Budget Data, March 1977" (March 20, 1977; processed), p. 22.

a. Converted to 1978 dollars using index for Navy operations and maintenance appropriations derived from data provided by the Office of the Assistant Secretary of Defense (Comptroller), March 1977.

Maintenance

The Department of Defense employs over 150,000 workers and spends over $4 billion in government-owned shipyards, aircraft overhaul facilities, and other depot maintenance activities. It is thus as large an industrial employer as firms ranking among the top ten in employment in the country.[19] These maintenance facilities are, in effect, factories that rebuild ships, aircraft and aircraft engines, tanks and other combat vehicles, missiles and other ordnance, as well as major subsystems and components. They often possess the physical facilities and the skilled labor force needed to manufacture as well as maintain such equipment and have at times engaged in production.

RISING OVERHAUL COSTS. The cost of military equipment maintenance is rising. For example, the total cost of overhauling Navy ships in fiscal 1978 is expected to top $1.5 billion, compared with about $397 million in 1968 (see table 4-3); and the real cost per overhaul has increased more than fivefold. Of course, some real cost increase is to be expected: ships are becoming larger and more complex; a growing proportion of

19. See *Department of Defense Appropriations for 1977*, Hearings before a Subcommittee of the House Committee on Appropriations, 94:2 (GPO, 1976), pt. 3, p. 655, and *Department of Defense Appropriations for Fiscal Year 1978*, Hearings before the Senate Committee on Appropriations, 95:1 (GPO, 1977) pt. 3, p. 46. In addition, the Department of Defense spends about $2 billion for depot maintenance in contractor facilities. Information on industrial organizations from *Fortune* (May 1977), pp. 366–67.

the fleet is nuclear-powered;[20] and recent overhauls have included repairs that had been deferred earlier. All three factors would give rise to greater overhaul costs. Yet such increases should have been at least partly offset by improvements in the general condition of the fleet as older ships were decommissioned and the average age declined by about 20 percent over the period.[21]

Moreover, if dramatic cost increases can be explained by changes in the composition of the fleet or increasing complexity even within the same type of ship, the increases should have been foreseeable, to some extent at least, when decisions were made on fleet composition and the procurement of more complex weapon systems and ships. If the cost of complexity is being systematically underestimated, maintenance costs can be expected to continue to climb as the military services shift to even more complicated systems.

There is some evidence that increases are not limited to the demands of a changing fleet composition. For example, the cost of overhauling the guided missile frigate *Joseph Strauss* in fiscal 1978 is estimated at $17.9 million, compared with $10.9 million for overhauling the same ship three years ago; the corresponding figures for the frigate *Sample* are $11.1 million and $6.1 million, respectively.[22] Since fiscal 1978 figures are budget estimates, the actual differences are likely to be even larger. It is possible, of course, that overhauls planned for fiscal 1978 are necessarily more extensive than those done three years earlier on the same ships; the additional requirements would have to be substantial, however, to account for the 35 to 50 percent real growth indicated by the figures quoted.

Such increases are limited neither to ships nor to the Navy. In 1977, the Air Force and Navy presented to Congress data on the cost of overhauling airframes, aircraft engines, and other equipment. Increases of 50 percent or more over a three-year period were not unusual.[23]

But a continued rise is not inevitable if maintenance policies are im-

20. Limiting the comparison to nonnuclear ships would reduce the increase to about 350 percent. The cost of overhauling nuclear ships has itself increased substantially in the last few years.

21. According to an estimate provided in September 1977 by the Office of the Chief of Naval Operations, the average age of the fleet has declined to 13.8 years in 1978, compared with 17.5 years in 1968.

22. *Department of Defense Appropriations for 1977*, House Hearings, pt. 3, p. 675, and *Department of Defense Appropriations for Fiscal Year 1978*, Senate Hearings, pt. 3, p. 763.

23. *Department of Defense Appropriations for 1978*, Senate Hearings, pt. 3, pp. 285–95.

proved. Theoretically, maintenance schedules are related to age of ships, hours of use of aircraft and engines, the time missiles have spent "on the shelf," the mileage of ground vehicles, and the like. The factors used by the services are based on engineering standards and past experience. Yet little is known about the relation between the frequency of major maintenance and the effectiveness of the overall force. In the past, the frequency and duration of overhauls have varied widely because of fiscal or operational pressures.

CHANGING MAINTENANCE PATTERNS. Current depot maintenance cycles and associated man-hours of work do not appear to be based on systematic analysis of the relation between maintenance and safety or operational effectiveness. On the contrary, Navy studies have confirmed earlier findings by commercial airlines: depot maintenance at scheduled intervals based on elapsed time or flying hours is unnecessary and in some cases undesirable.[24] This evidence led to the adoption of a strategy developed by the airlines called "reliability-centered maintenance." Rather than doing maintenance at scheduled intervals, inspections are first performed to determine whether the maintenance is necessary. The system has been described by a defense official:

This strategy requires that an engineering analysis of the specific equipment be performed to identify the risk of failure of a particular component, the feasibility of detecting impending failure, and the efficiency of alternative maintenance actions. Through a sequence of "logic" steps, maintenance actions that contribute to retaining or restoring equipment reliability are identified and scheduled. Other maintenance actions are eliminated.

With these analysis techniques, the airlines were able to significantly reduce scheduled inspections, removals, and repairs without adversely impacting their excellent safety record. Corresponding reductions were achieved both in the cost of scheduled maintenance and in equipment downtime.[25]

In essence, this maintenance strategy attempts to strike a balance between operational effectiveness and safety. Some equipment, especially complex equipment, tends to fail at the same rate after preventive maintenance as before. Indeed, it has been demonstrated that some aircraft engines are less reliable *after* overhaul than at any other time.[26]

24. See William Lavallee and Others, "Aircraft Engine Maintenance Study" (Center for Naval Analyses, September 1975; processed), and William Lavallee, "Aircraft Periodic Depot Level Maintenance Study" (Center for Naval Analyses, November 1974; processed).

25. Joseph G. Turke, "It Isn't the Cost; It's the Upkeep," *Defense Management Journal*, vol. 13 (July 1977), p. 6.

26. Lavallee and others, "Aircraft Engine Maintenance Study," p. 17.

Recent changes in the maintenance schedule of Navy P-3 antisubmarine warfare aircraft provide an illustration of potential savings. As a result of refinements in aircraft maintenance programs, the time between overhauls for the P-3 has been extended from thirty-six to sixty months and the amount of work done will be less by 2,000 man-hours per aircraft.[27] Similarly, the Air Force has extended its cycles under a program known as "controlled interval extension."[28]

The Navy has also changed the overhaul cycles for some strategic submarines, extending them from six to nine years and, under budget pressure, extended many cycles for surface ships.[29] But its major new effort, known as the Ship Support Improvement Program, to assess its ship maintenance strategies more systematically should realize considerable savings, if experience with nuclear submarines is any indication.[30] When and how much will be saved, however, is unclear. Citing the large backlog of ships awaiting overhaul, former Secretary of Defense Donald H. Rumsfeld has estimated that it will take five or six years before the fleet attains a satisfactory matériel condition, after which savings can be expected.[31]

Nonetheless, in general terms, Secretary Rumsfeld has indicated that the savings associated with all ongoing efforts to improve the efficiency of the overall Department of Defense logistics establishment would amount to some $2 billion a year.[32] To the extent that the military services can apply the improvements they have already made more widely and at an accelerated pace, the savings could be realized sooner and could be larger.

CONTROLLING OVERHEAD COSTS. Apparent increases in overhead costs also warrant attention. Total civilian employment in naval shipyards, for example, declined by 25 percent since 1964 and the number of blue-collar workers has been reduced by 27 percent, but the number of white-

27. See Cyril T. Faulders, Jr., "The Analytical Maintenance Program: No More 'Maintenance as Usual'," *Defense Management Journal,* vol. 13 (July 1977), pp. 18–19.

28. *Department of Defense Appropriations for Fiscal Year 1978,* Senate Hearings, pt. 3, p. 293.

29. For a brief discussion of this program, see *Department of Defense Appropriations for 1978,* Hearings before a Subcommittee of the Committee on Appropriations, 95:1 (GPO, 1977), pt. 1, p. 451.

30. *Department of Defense Appropriations, Fiscal Year 1976,* Hearings before the Senate Committee on Appropriations, 94:1 (GPO, 1975), pt. 3, p. 1035.

31. Department of Defense, *Annual Defense Department Report, FY 1978,* Report of Secretary of Defense Donald H. Rumsfeld to the Congress on FY 1978 Budget, FY 1979 Authorization Request, and FY 1978–1982 Defense Programs (GPO, 1977), p. 277.

32. Ibid., p. 275.

Table 4-4. Indexes of Overhead and Man-Day Costs, Selected Naval Shipyards, Fiscal Year 1976[a]

Shipyard	Overhead index[b]	Man-day index[b]
Charleston, South Carolina	136	117
Portsmouth, New Hampshire	130	112
Mare Island, California	124	118
Pearl Harbor, Hawaii	124	119
Norfolk, Virginia	124	104
Philadelphia, Pennsylvania	120	108
Long Beach, California	106	104
Puget Sound, Washington	100	100

Source: Based on *Department of Defense Appropriations, Fiscal Year 1978*, Hearings before the Senate Committee on Appropriations, 95:1 (GPO, 1977), pt. 3, p. 283.
a. Cost per man-day includes both overhead and labor charges.
b. Puget Sound = 100.

collar employees has been reduced by only 12 percent.[33] There are also wide variations among shipyards in the cost of providing the same services. In fiscal 1976 overhead rates at some shipyards were as much as 36 percent above those of the lowest-cost yard, while man-day rates (labor plus overhead) varied by almost 20 percent (see table 4-4). Aggregate measures such as these oversimplify, but they nonetheless serve the useful purpose of identifying possible differences in the efficiency with which shipyards operate. More detailed comparisons among naval yards and between naval yards and private yards could lead to better management practices. Similar differences are shown by the Air Force and Navy for their depots that overhaul aircraft and engines. Part of the variation from depot to depot and yard to yard can be explained by regional variation in wage rates and by the complexity of the workload (which may lead to higher labor costs); but part must also be attributed to differences in efficiency.

Supply Operations

Each service operates a complex network of supply depots to keep its forces stocked with parts and equipment necessary to maintain desired

33. Although white-collar employment does not precisely represent overhead costs, an examination of the source data shows it to be a reasonable proxy. For example, of all blue-collar workers employed by naval shipyards, 83 percent are assigned to production departments whereas only 14 percent of white-collar workers are found there. See Department of the Navy, "Statistics of Naval Shipyards" (Sea Systems Command, June 30, 1964; processed), and Department of the Navy, "Statistics of Naval Shipyards" (Sea Systems Command, December 31, 1976; processed).

levels of readiness. The Defense Logistics Agency is also responsible for the management of supplies common to all services, such as medical goods and petroleum. The people employed in these operations buy, store, distribute, manage, and control supplies, equipment, components, and spare parts. The number of people required depends on the location of forces, the amount of equipment in the forces, type of equipment, where it is located, how intensively it is used in peacetime, and the desired level of combat readiness. The determination of manpower requirements for supply operations lends itself to well-established inventory and processing methods and well-developed workload measurement techniques.

Yet, through the years, each military department has established its own supply network largely in isolation from the other departments. Although each service has periodically analyzed and improved its own supply system, little has been done to evaluate the defense supply system as a whole. An analysis by the Department of Defense Matériel Distribution System Study Group scheduled for completion in 1978 promises to do just this. The results of this study, being made under the auspices of the joint logistics commanders, should start to provide answers to some tough questions: What constitutes the peacetime and surge requirements for the supply system? Do redundancies exist? Can automation lead to greater efficiency? Does it make sense to increase dependence on commercial supply support? When such questions are answered, the task of assessing the appropriateness of employing 122,000 people in defense supply activities can begin.

Other Logistics Support

Various activities such as technical documentation, printing, engineering and testing, contractors' technical representation, and procurement are included in the category termed "other logistics support." They are difficult to describe in a way that would help a top-level decisionmaker exert broad policy control over them. While these activities undoubtedly contribute to the readiness of U.S. forces, their relation to national security is even harder to define than that of supply and maintenance activities. Indeed, it is difficult to estimate the impact on military capability of changes in the level of employment in these activities. Until these functions are better understood, both inside and outside the Pentagon, they will remain subject to arbitrary reductions.

THE FOREGOING discussion supports the conclusion that the defense civilian work force is larger than necessary to meet U.S. national security requirements. It is widely recognized that the armed forces are operating more installations than they feel are required for strictly military purposes. That some bases are more efficient than others is also obvious. Finally, how military effectiveness will be affected by changes in civilian employment in defense logistics activities needs to be assessed. The size of potential savings, however, is difficult to estimate. The results of future analyses, some of which are already under way within the Department of Defense, will be required before confident and precise estimates of possible manpower savings can be made.

CHAPTER FIVE

THE MILITARY-CIVILIAN MIX

Bureaucratic and political factors aside, on technical grounds alone, what is an appropriate balance between military and civilian employees in the Department of Defense? An answer depends on cost and effectiveness. If it costs more to fill some billets with uniformed employees than with civilians and if the jobs can be done by civilians without risk to U.S. national security, it follows that if those billets are filled by military personnel the nation is paying more than is necessary to field its armed forces. The converse is also true if there are civilian jobs that could be done more cheaply by the military.

This chapter analyzes the relative cost of military and federal civilian employees, examines current policies limiting their interchangeability, and what might happen should these policies be changed.

Comparing the Costs of Military and Civilian Manpower

With the end of military conscription and with the adoption of strong incentives to attract military volunteers, a great deal of attention has been directed in recent years to the relative pay of military and civilian personnel. Few cost comparisons have sparked so much controversy among defense analysts. The importance of that debate should not be minimized, yet direct payroll costs are but one element that needs to be considered in choosing among alternative types of manpower. It is more important to compare the *total* annual cost to the government attributable to a particular billet or assignment filled by a military incumbent with the corresponding total cost of the same billet or assignment filled by a federal civilian incumbent. In other words, what are the total budgetary implications of converting a military position, say, at the E-5 level, to a civilian position, or of converting a GS-7 civilian billet to a military job? As straightforward and as important as that question is, there is little agreement on an answer; there does not even appear to be an agreed-upon method for making the calculation.

In recent years, since the comparability pay rule has been extended to military personnel, and particularly with the advent of the all-volunteer force, some analysts have come to believe that it is less costly to fill a job with a federal civilian than with a uniformed employee. Indeed, the Department of Defense shares this view:

> Least cost is an implied criterion in the guidance concerning military-civilian determinations because civilians currently are generally less costly than military manpower. This results primarily from the fact that military personnel generate more secondary support requirements than do civilians. . . . Further, additional backup (or pipeline) positions are included in military strength as trainees, transients, patients, and prisoners.[1]

Calculating Costs

What constitutes the total annual costs that can be attributed to a particular billet? Far more is involved than the amount that the incumbent receives as a wage or salary; account must also be taken of a variety of fringe benefits as well as the indirect costs associated with keeping a billet filled. For the military, this means imputing the cost of such things as non-contributory retirement and health care, and for both military and civilians it means allocating support and pipeline costs (training, travel, and the like) to each billet. Needless to say, there is little agreement on the appropriate cost of fringe benefits for the military and civilian employees and even less on what indirect costs should be included and how they should be allocated. And, even when agreement is reached on these issues, there remains the question of how to link military and civilian grades.

The analysis here assembles costs in three categories: compensation, pipeline, and indirect. They are summarized below; detailed descriptions are found in appendix C.

COMPENSATION COSTS. There is much disagreement about what constitutes compensation. Part of the difficulty arises from the complexities of the military pay system, which—in addition to cash payments—includes an array of benefits, some of which are in kind, some deferred, and

1. Office of the Assistant Secretary of Defense (Manpower and Reserve Affairs), "The Mix of the Defense Labor Force" (1976; processed), p. 6.

others conditional.[2] And the civilian compensation system, while more straightforward, is not without its own contentious properties.

Included for military personnel are (1) the four elements that constitute "regular military compensation": basic pay, quarters allowance, subsistence allowance, and the federal tax advantage accruing because allowances are not taxable; (2) the major fringe benefits, retirement and health care; and (3) compensation-related elements such as unemployment compensation and life insurance. (Items such as enlistment bonuses, flight pay, and sea-duty pay, which are excluded from this category, are discussed below. Also excluded, for reasons discussed in appendix C, is the government contribution to social security.)

For civilians, included in this category are base pay, overtime and holiday pay, life insurance, retirement, health benefits, unemployment compensation, and workmen's compensation. Compensation costs for selected military and civilian grades are shown in table 5-1.

For both military and civilians, retirement costs have been based on a fully funded retirement system. Thus a fixed percentage of base pay is calculated, which if set aside annually in an interest-bearing fund would accrue at a rate such that the accumulated principal and interest would just pay off the future benefits as they became due until the last beneficiary died. If an annual real wage increase of 1.5 percent and a 2.5 percent real return on the investment funds are assumed, the fixed percentage of base pay—"normal cost" in the idiom of the actuary—is roughly 27 percent of salary for civilians (of which the employee now contributes 7 percent) and about 36 percent of basic pay for military employees. These economic assumptions, widely applied within the administration, are used here only for illustration. It is recognized that the result is extremely sensitive to the assumptions; however, within a reasonable range, alternative assumptions would not change the relationships shown in table 5-1, since the relative effects on military and civilian employees would be approximately the same.[3]

PIPELINE COSTS. In addition to the employees on the job, the military services also maintain a pool of people to offset those absent from their jobs while undergoing training, traveling between assignments, and the

2. For a description of the military pay system and its problems, see Martin Binkin, *The Military Pay Muddle* (Brookings Institution, 1975).

3. Sensitivity to interest rates is particularly striking. For example, if the real interest rate is assumed to be 1.5 rather than 2.5 percent, the normal cost for military personnel becomes 48 percent.

Table 5-1. Average Annual Compensation Costs for Selected Military
and Civilian Grades, Fiscal Year 1978[a]
Dollars

Military		Civilian			
		General schedule		Wage Board[b]	
Grade	Amount	Grade	Amount	Grade	Amount
Officer					
O-9	75,900	GS-17	58,300	WS-17	36,600
O-7	60,100	GS-15	51,800	WS-15	33,900
O-5	41,800	GS-13	37,800	WL-13	25,500
O-3	29,400	GS-11	26,100	WL-11	24,800
O-1	17,100	GS-9	21,500	WL-9	22,300
		GS-7	17,900	WG-7	19,000
Enlisted		GS-5	14,800	WG-5	17,200
E-9	29,400	GS-3	11,600	WG-3	15,600
E-7	22,100	GS-1	9,400	WG-1	14,300
E-5	15,800				
E-3	12,100				

Source: See appendix C.

a. Compensation costs for military personnel include basic pay, quarters and subsistence allowances, tax advantage, and fringe benefits considered to be a form of compensation (for example, retirement and medical benefits, unemployment compensation, and veterans' educational benefits); for civilians, they include base pay, overtime and holiday pay, life insurance, retirement and health benefits, unemployment compensation, and workmen's compensation.

b. Two or more grades in each of the three Wage Board schedules are shown for illustrative purposes. See appendix A for a description of civilian categories.

like. The size of this so-called pipeline is obviously related to the amount of training conducted and the frequency of reassignment. The pipeline associated with military personnel is significantly larger than for civilian personnel as a consequence of the different nature of the two systems (see chapter 3). How great this difference is can be seen in table 5-2. Training costs have been allocated to each grade in such a way as to reflect the average yearly value of the training investment in an individual in that grade, on the assumption that the cost of each type of training is amortized uniformly over the remaining career of the recipient. Travel costs (other than those related to training), such as those associated with overseas moves and operational reassignments, are allocated uniformly on a per capita basis. Since the civilian personnel system is "open," training costs are much lower and have been allocated in a somewhat different manner, as explained in appendix C.

INDIRECT SUPPORT COSTS. The Department of Defense provides a variety of support services, the cost of which should be allocated to its employees: commissaries and exchanges; recreation, welfare, and morale

Table 5-2. Average Annual Pipeline Costs for Selected Military and Civilian Grades, Fiscal Year 1978[a]

Dollars

		Civilian			
Military		General schedule		Wage Board[b]	
Grade	Amount	Grade	Amount	Grade	Amount
Officer					
O-9	10,200	GS-17	2,300	WS-17	570
O-7	9,500	GS-15	1,600	WS-15	520
O-5	8,300	GS-13	1,100	WL-13	330
O-3	6,100	GS-11	900	WL-11	270
O-1	4,000	GS-9	750	WL-9	230
		GS-7	600	WG-7	200
Enlisted		GS-5	450	WG-5	170
E-9	3,100	GS-3	110	WG-3	20
E-7	2,700	GS-1	60	WG-1	20
E-5	2,300				
E-3	1,700				

Source: See appendix C.

a. Pipeline costs are those directly associated with training and relocating personnel and with offsetting the time lost by patients and prisoners.

b. Two or more grades in each of the three Wage Board schedules are shown for illustrative purposes.

services; preparing and serving food; and overhead services allocated to training activities. The bulk of the cost of these services is attributed to military personnel, as the comparison in table 5-3 illustrates. It is important to note that, unlike compensation and pipeline costs, indirect support costs do not vary proportionately with changes in employment levels. In other words, the elimination of a small number of positions on a base would have little impact on the cost of providing base services. Indirect support costs should therefore be included in cost comparisons only for major changes in employment.

EQUIVALENT GRADES. The effect on costs of substituting one type of labor for another depends heavily on the grade levels of the respective employees. In the past, various schemes have been discussed for establishing equivalent military and civilian grades, but as yet no hard-and-fast rules have been developed. In the third Quadrennial Review of Military Compensation in 1976, a Department of Defense study group evaluated several methods of determining the comparability of jobs in the military and civilian grade structures. One of these methods, developed by Hay Associates, uses a point-count system to compare the content of both

Table 5-3. Average Annual Indirect Support Costs for Selected Military and Civilian Grades, Fiscal Year 1978

Dollars

Military		Civilian			
		General schedule		Wage Board[a]	
Grade	Amount	Grade	Amount	Grade	Amount
Officer					
O-9	1,570	GS-17	430	WS-17	60
O-7	1,660	GS-15	350	WS-15	60
O-5	1,820	GS-13	250	WL-13	40
O-3	1,350	GS-11	210	WL-11	40
O-1	780	GS-9	180	WL-9	30
Enlisted		GS-7	150	WG-7	40
		GS-5	120	WG-5	30
E-9	1,650	GS-3	60	WG-3	30
E-7	1,650	GS-1	40	WG-1	30
E-5	1,300				
E-3	870				

Source: See appendix C.
a. Two or more grades in each of three Wage Board schedules are shown for illustrative purposes.

similar and dissimilar jobs.[4] Each job is evaluated by the problem-solving skills required and by the degree of accountability. The point counts are used to identify civil service grade levels whose median job content is above and below the median job content of the military grade being evaluated, thus locating the military grade in relation to two civilian grades. The job content of a military grade is then assigned to a point on a percentage scale between the two civil service grades with the next lower and next higher median job content. The results for six military grades (three officer and three enlisted) are shown in table 5-4.

COST COMPARISONS. The results of the cost analysis and the linkages discussed above are brought together in table 5-5. When only compensation costs are compared, military personnel always cost less than blue-collar civilians, primarily as a consequence of the anomalies in the blue-collar pay system mentioned in chapter 2. The relative cost of equivalent military and white-collar civilian employees, on the other hand, depends on grade; at grade levels 0-1 and 0-5, for example, military personnel ap-

4. Office of the Secretary of Defense, "Third Quadrennial Review of Military Compensation: Staff Studies and Selected Supporting Papers," vol. 8 (December 1976; processed), pp. ES-8–12.

Table 5-4. Comparison of Median Job Content between Military Personnel and Federal Civilian Employees at Selected Grade Levels

Military grade	Relation of military grade to civilian grades				Point on percentage scale of military grade between civilian grades[a]	
	White-collar		Blue-collar		White-collar	Blue-collar
	Lower	Higher	Lower	Higher		
Officer						
O-5	GS-14	GS-15	...	...	24	...
O-2	GS-9	GS-11	...	...	14	...
O-1	GS-7	GS-9	...	...	54	...
Enlisted						
E-7	GS-7	GS-9	WS-9	WS-10	18	37
E-5	GS-5	GS-7	WG-8	WG-10	26	84
E-3	GS-3	GS-5	WG-3	WG-5	13	79

Source: Office of the Secretary of Defense, "Third Quadrennial Review of Military Compensation: Staff Studies and Selected Supporting Papers," vol. 8 (December 1976; processed).

a. Expressed as a percentage of the difference between those civilian grades with lower and higher median job content than the military grade under consideration. For example, the median job complexity of a military grade O-5 is 24 percent of the way from the median GS-14 to the median GS-15.

pear to cost about 14 percent and 9 percent less, respectively, than civilians, while at most other grades civilians cost less, ranging from 1 percent at E-3 to about 16 percent at E-7.

When pipeline costs are taken into account, the relative cost advantage of white-collar civilians across all grades becomes apparent and, while blue-collar workers continue to be more expensive than their military counterparts, the differences are narrower. The inclusion of indirect support costs widens the disparity between military personnel and white-collar civilians; at established linkage points, the cost advantage of employing white-collar civilians ranges from about 5 percent at grade O-1 to 27 percent at grade E-7. Finally, the introduction of indirect support costs further diminishes, but does not close, the gap between enlisted personnel and blue-collar civilians; the latter are from 3 to 24 percent more expensive than their military counterparts.

These results should be interpreted with caution. The methodology is an attempt to simplify a complex and poorly defined relationship and it has inherent limitations. First, the figures represent average rather than marginal costs. For example, the method used here allocates retirement costs as a percentage of pay, regardless of grade, ignoring the fact that the probability of reaching retirement eligibility increases with grade and

Table 5-5. Total Average Annual Costs Attributable to Selected Military Grades and Equivalent Federal Civilian Grades, Fiscal Year 1978

Dollars

Military grade	Compensation cost			Compensation plus pipeline costs			Total cost[a]		
		Civilian			Civilian			Civilian	
	Military	White-collar	Blue-collar	Military	White-collar	Blue-collar	Military	White-collar	Blue-collar
Officer									
O-5	41,800	45,900	...	49,600	47,300	...	51,900	47,700	...
O-2	23,500	22,100	...	27,900	22,900	...	29,000	23,100	...
O-1	17,100	19,800	...	20,800	20,500	...	21,900	20,700	...
Enlisted									
E-7	22,100	18,500	26,900	24,600	19,200	27,300	26,400	19,400	27,300
E-5	15,800	15,600	21,000	17,900	16,100	21,300	19,400	16,300	21,300
E-3	12,100	12,000	17,900	13,600	12,200	18,100	14,600	12,300	18,100

Source: See appendix C.

a. Compensation plus pipeline plus indirect support costs.

varies according to skill. The bias thus introduced could be significant when comparing retirement costs among military grades; it is less important when comparing military and civilian employees.

Second, variations in cost that occur among occupations and geographical areas are not considered. For example, special and premium payments made to military personnel in certain skills are not reflected in these comparisons. Since their pay rates are locally determined, the costs of blue-collar workers vary geographically. These differences would have to be taken into account when comparing costs of conversions in a particular occupation or in a particular location.

Third, the cost comparisons depend on the validity of the assumed linkages. The consequences of applying job content values above and below the median values used in the illustration are shown in appendix C; for the most part, while the magnitude of the differences change, the general conclusions do not. Regardless of analyses of job content, the cost implications of conversions would depend on the grades that are actually involved, which in turn depend on how conversions are implemented by the responsible agency.[5]

Finally, the list of cost items probably does not include all the elements that should be considered as manpower-related expenses. For example, several "hidden" elements, excluded from the comparison, would raise both military and civilian manpower costs. In much the same fashion that support costs are allocated to military personnel, it could be argued that costs such as those associated with national scholarship and loan programs and with income tax reductions for medical expenses should be imputed to federal civilians. By the same token, except for the cost of the GI Bill, veterans' benefits have not been included. The costs of the excluded elements are difficult to measure precisely, but they would tend to cancel each other out.

Thus it should not be concluded that the conversion of *any* military billet, say, at the E-7 grade level to a civilian position at the equivalent median grade would result in a reduction of $7,000 annually, as table 5-5 suggests. For a specific conversion, the marginal cost associated with a particular position would differ from the average cost shown to an extent dependent on the characteristics of the billet in question. In general, the

5. See Roy E. Smoker, "Economic Cost as a Military Essentiality Criterion," Paper presented to the Rand Conference on Defense Manpower, Santa Monica, California (February 1976; processed), pp. 27–28, which discusses the results of Air Force experience with civilian substitution.

more complex the tasks associated with a particular job, the greater the amount of skill training required, and the greater the cost of the military incumbent. Thus, for highly skilled positions, the marginal savings from converting the E-7 to an equivalent civilian grade is likely to exceed $7,000 and make the case for civilian substitution even more persuasive. Alternatively, for positions requiring little training, the marginal savings would be less than $7,000. The number of cases in which the marginal cost of an E-7 would be *less* than the marginal cost of a civilian at the equivalent grade is hard to assess, but it is likely to be small.

Therefore, in a great majority of cases, conversions from military to white-collar civilian personnel would result in long-term budgetary savings whose precise magnitude would depend on the nature of the billets being converted. By similar logic, the analysis suggests that the substitution of military personnel for blue-collar civilians, at current pay rates, might also lower costs.

Looking to the Future[6]

The relative cost of sustaining military personnel and civilians under current conditions is likely to be less important financially than the opportunity cost associated with maintaining existing military recruitment policies in the face of developing demographic and economic trends. Doubts are growing about whether this nation, despite recent large increases in monetary incentives, will be able to sustain an all-volunteer force of appropriate quality.

Two disquieting factors on the horizon are the imminent decline in the number of young men in the population as the postwar baby boom runs its course and the diminishing proportion likely to volunteer as the economy improves.

In the years ahead, as the effects of dwindling birthrates in the 1960s begin to be felt, the number of young men reaching the age of eighteen each year will decline sharply from present levels, dropping 15 percent by 1985 and over 25 percent by 1992. If the armed forces remain at their present size, recruiting will be more difficult; instead of having to attract one of every six males, as is now the case, the military services eventually will have to attract one of every four. Moreover, assuming that the economy continues to recover, the number of male high school graduates

6. A more extensive discussion of this issue appears in Martin Binkin and Shirley J. Bach, *Women and the Military* (Brookings Institution, 1977).

attracted to military service could become disturbingly small and require an increase in military pay relative to civilian pay in order to meet recruitment needs. If this is not done, if military pay raises only match civilian pay raises, by 1981 the services will be fortunate to attract 80 percent of their stated needs for high school graduates; by 1985 that figure is likely to decrease to 63 percent. The greater the economic recovery, the greater the shortfall.

There are, of course, many options for improving recruitment, only one of which is to grant across-the-board increases in military pay. To illustrate what might be involved if that strategem were followed, it is estimated that just to continue to attract the number of male high-school graduates who volunteered in 1976—225,000—the military payroll would have to be almost $6 billion a year greater by 1982 than is currently projected for that year. Over the 1978–82 period, cumulative extra pay costs would be $14 billion.[7] Were the economy to experience an even stronger recovery than is assumed here, and thus if unemployment were to fall even more, prospects would be greater for even larger shortfalls, and hence for even higher costs to attract recruits of consistent quality. If this occurs, the present financial advantage of replacing military personnel with white-collar civilians would be even greater, and it is possible that the costs of military personnel would overtake those of blue-collar civilians. Accordingly, it is important to examine current policies limiting the substitution of civilians for military personnel and what might happen should those policies be changed.

Potential Utilization under Current Policies

The ground rules that govern the relative numbers of military and civilian employees in the armed forces are imprecise, and the rationale underlying the determination of the current composition is unclear. Whether combat forces—for example, Army or Marine Corps infantrymen, naval destroyer crews, and Air Force strategic bomber crews—should be military or civilian is obviously not at issue. And few would

7. Derived from data provided by the U.S. Congress, Congressional Budget Office, January 1977. Projections based on a pay elasticity of 1.00 and unemployment elasticity of 0.45. Thus a 1.0 percent change in military pay relative to civilian pay and a 2.2 percent change in youth employment are each assumed to produce a 1 percent change in enlistments of male high-school graduates.

doubt that those who directly support the combat forces and who are expected to operate in a combat zone should be uniformed personnel.

Even when agreement is reached on this obvious point—that "combat forces" should be composed of military personnel—a question remains: what constitutes the "combat forces?" The distinctions are not as sharp as they appear. Must crews flying and servicing airlift aircraft similar in configuration to those used commercially, such as the C-5, be military? Must naval support ships, such as oilers and tenders, be manned by naval personnel? And where to draw the line between military and civilian personnel combat support functions becomes more difficult to judge when it is recalled that U.S. combat forces currently deployed rely on foreign national civilians for certain forms of support.

Moreover, the distinctions become even more blurred when one takes into account the need for a rotation base (billets reserved in the United States to give personnel a respite from overseas duty) and the criterion of "military necessity" (billets reserved for military personnel for reasons of discipline, security, and the like).

Because so much depends on how combat is defined and on "military judgment," the task of determining which jobs require a military incumbent would be difficult even if data on individual jobs were available. The approach taken here leaves the combat question aside by assuming that all military personnel now deployed outside the territorial United States, aboard naval vessels, or in units now in the United States but intended for overseas deployment in a contingency are in billets that require uniformed incumbents.

Deployed and Deployable Billets[8]

Estimating the size of the deployed forces is straightforward. At the end of fiscal 1977, the Army, Marine Corps, and Air Force had about 206,000, 26,000, and 87,000 enlisted troops, respectively, deployed overseas; and the Navy had about 275,000 sailors aboard ships or overseas.

The number of billets in units now in the United States but earmarked for deployment (so-called deployable billets) is more difficult to estimate. For the Army, the number of positions in "table of organization and equipment" (TO&E) units provides a reasonable approximation. Loosely

8. Based on data obtained by the authors from the Department of Defense between June 1977 and April 1978.

defined, these are combat, combat support, and combat service support units expected to deploy during wartime. In contrast are "table of distribution allowances" (TDA) units that, for the most part, would remain in the United States. By this rule of thumb, about 230,000 of a total of some 330,000 Army enlisted jobs in the United States are in units scheduled for wartime deployment.

Naval shore establishment units are not earmarked for deployment. By current standards, naval vessels are manned at full strength; moreover, within limits, shortages could be met by mobilizing trained reservists.

Since the primary mission of the Marine Corps is amphibious warfare, the bulk of Marine units embark periodically aboard amphibious ships. In fact, about 99,000 enlisted billets (72 percent of the total) are in combat divisions, aircraft wings, force troops, and force service regiments, which collectively compose the Fleet Marine Forces (FMF). Thus, in addition to the 26,000 members of the FMF deployed forward, about 73,000 enlisted Marines are in units in the territorial United States that would be likely to be deployed in an emergency.

The number of Air Force enlisted personnel in units that might be deployed is the most difficult to ascertain. Much would depend on assumptions about how long a war might last, expected attrition, and the like. Under worst-case situations—a protracted war in Europe and a simultaneous minor conflict, say, in the Middle East—the Air Force would be likely to consider its entire force to be deployable. Ostensibly, personnel are already positioned at foreign bases to support combat flying units that would be deployed overseas in wartime. However, assuming that *all* Air Force personnel not already deployed who are associated with the tactical air mission (fighter, attack, and airlift aircraft) and with communications and intelligence, including headquarters and base operations manpower—a total of 200,000—were considered deployable, there would still be 128,000 enlisted men in Air Force units who would be expected to remain in the United States.

Rotation Requirements[9]

To ensure that military personnel are not required to spend a disproportionate share of their time at sea, in remote allocations, or on similar

9. Based on data in Office of the Assistant Secretary of Defense (Manpower and Reserve Affairs), Central All-Volunteer Task Force, "Civilian Substitution" (October 1972; processed), Tab C.

duty, a certain number of billets must be made available in the United States so that personnel can be rotated between assignments. The size of the so-called rotation base, which depends largely on the size and location of deployments and the length of duty tours, varies by service. For example, in 1972 the services estimated their rotation needs as follows (expressed as a percentage of their overseas or sea-duty deployments): Army, 45 percent; Navy, 27 percent; Marine Corps, 269 percent; and Air Force, 196 percent. In other words, the Navy reserved one billet in their shore establishment for every four sea-duty billets while the Marine Corps reserved over five positions in the United States for every two located overseas. The relatively large rotation base of the Marine Corps and the Air Force arises from the practice in these services of stationing personnel in the United States for longer periods than the Army and the Navy.

The enlisted rotation requirements for each service, estimated by applying the above percentages to current deployments, are as follows: Army, 93,000; Navy, 74,000; Marine Corps, 70,000; Air Force, 171,000. Except for the Navy, these requirements might be met in part by rotating personnel between deployed units and deployable units. The extent to which this could be done would depend on how well the skill and grade specifications of the jobs in each category could be matched with the skills and grades of the personnel being reassigned. In the 1972 study, the Army estimated that 44 percent of its deployable billets could be used to satisfy rotation needs, the Air Force estimated 83 percent, and the Marine Corps 63 percent. If those proportions are representative, the Army would not have to reserve any additional positions for rotation, the Navy would have to set aside 74,000, the Marine Corps 24,000, and the Air Force 5,000.

Potential Substitution

The combined effects of the above estimates are shown in table 5-6. The number of military enlisted billets not accounted for by deployed, deployable, and rotation requirements differs among the services. The Army and Air Force have the greatest number of billets not thus accounted for: about 23 percent of all Army and 30 percent of all Air Force military enlisted jobs are not explained by the factors considered so far. By similar logic, about 75,000 military jobs now filled by officers should be scrutinized.

Table 5-6. Maximum Potential Substitution of Civilian for Military Enlisted Billets, by Service, Fiscal Year 1977

Thousands of billets

Category	Army	Navy	Marine Corps	Air Force	Total
Total number of enlisted billets	**567**	**382**	**138**	**415**	**1,502**
Number of deployed billets[a]	206	275	26	87	594
Number of deployable billets[b]	230	...	73	200	503
Number of billets reserved for rotation[c]	...	74	24	5	103
Subtotal	436	349	123	292	1,200
Maximum number of billets that might be filled by civilians	**131**	**33**	**15**	**123**	**302**
Percentage of total	*23*	*9*	*11*	*30*	*20*

Source: Authors' estimates based on discussion in text.
a. Military billets outside the United States and its territories or aboard naval vessels.
b. Military billets in units in the United States expected to deploy in a contingency, including TO&E units in the Army, Fleet Marine Force units in the Marine Corps, and *all* Air Force units in Programs II (Tactical Air), III (Communications and Intelligence), and IV (Airlift).
c. Includes rotation requirements not met by using deployable billets in the United States; see text discussion.

Why do these 377,000 jobs require a military incumbent? The answer is not clear, but the military services are likely to explain it by referring to the "military necessity" terminology of the official rationale set forth in Department of Defense Directive 1100.4 (discussed in chapter 2): law, training, security, discipline, and the like. For example, it would be argued that those involved with recruiting and with some forms of training should be in the military. The number of jobs that appropriately are included in this category are difficult to estimate. A proper analysis would require access to a roster of detailed jobs and their specifications; even then, however, "military judgment" is likely to be the dominant criterion. If Pentagon estimates contained in the 1972 study remain valid, at the low extreme, about one-third of these positions would not strictly require a military incumbent; at most, perhaps one-half of the billets could be filled by either military or civilians.[10]

These modest estimates could be increased somewhat by relaxing some of the conservative assumptions of the foregoing analysis: the abnormally high rotation requirements for the Air Force and Marine Corps could be lowered, and the number of deployable Air Force billets may be larger than necessary. All told, however, such changes would be marginal, confined mainly to support activities, such as logistics, base services, and training.

10. Ibid., Tab C.

The extent of financial savings would, of course, depend on such factors as skill, grade, and the number of substitutions. Obviously, as matters stand, only those substitutions involving white-collar civilians would be likely to be profitable. For every 10,000 military jobs that could be filled by white-collar civilian employees, savings would approach $50 million a year.[11]

Potential Utilization under Revised Policies

To go much beyond the potential substitution outlined above would require fundamental changes in defense manpower policies. It would mean using civilians in units and under conditions that have traditionally been considered the military's exclusive domain.

Navy Fleet Support

Among the leading candidates is Navy fleet support. Manning support vessels with civilians is not a new concept. Indeed, the British Royal Fleet Auxiliary has been manned by civilians for many years. But it was not until 1971 that the U.S. Navy turned to its Military Sealift Command (MSC) to test the feasibility of using federal civilian employees. By early 1977, the MSC was operating seventeen ships in direct support of fleet commanders (eight oilers, four tugs, one refrigerated stores ship, and four ballistic missile submarine resupply ships). By most accounts, these ships are providing equal if not better service to the fleet at a lower cost than would be incurred if the ships were manned by military personnel. For example, by one estimate the cost of operating the *Taluga* (a fleet oiler) by MSC for one year was $3.3 million (in 1973 dollars) compared with the $5.3 million it would have cost had it been operated by full military crews.[12] More recently, a study to assess a proposal to transfer destroyer tenders and repair ships to MSC concluded:

> The concept of transferring ownership of destroyer tenders and repair ships to MSC is feasible. There is no reason that these ships, operated and maintained by MSC crews with embarked MILDEPTs [Military Departments],

11. Based on the assumption that most of the conversions would occur at the E-5 to E-8 grade levels in such occupations as communications and intelligence, medical and dental, and administration specialists and clerks.

12. Paul Stillwell, "A Navy Success: Support Ships Manned by Civilian Crews," *Armed Forces Journal* (July 1976), pp. 26, 28.

could not effectively perform the primary missions now assigned to Navy de-stroyer tenders and repair ships.[13]

Financial savings, according to the study, were estimated at $1 million a year for the *Gompers*-class tender, after one-time costs of about $5 million for modifications to accommodate MSC operating procedures and standards.[14]

How well do these civilian-manned ships perform? According to one firsthand observer:

Over a seven-month West Pac [Western Pacific Ocean] deployment, we were alongside MSC ships a dozen times—each time with the same results, the same superb performance. To a man, the wardroom developed a high regard for their operational capabilities, frankly to the detriment of our own com-missioned replenishment ships which never stood up well in a one-to-one com-parison alongside.[15]

Of concern to naval planners, however, is the risk of relying on federal civilian employees for essential fleet support in the event of a war or other military contingency. Such concern does not appear to be well founded. The observer quoted above added that "in MSC's 27-year existence, in-cluding the six years of Navy fleet support activity, command operations have never been hampered by strikes or work slowdowns."[16]

Of the sixty-odd active naval vessels now in the auxiliary category, the number that could be operated by federal civilians of the MSC without reducing the ability of the Navy to fulfill its worldwide commitments can only be speculated upon and deserves further analysis. Altogether, close to 30,000 military jobs are involved. The prospect of using civilians in seagoing billets is particularly attractive because it would also reduce the requirement to reserve military rotation billets in the shore establish-ment—billets that otherwise might be filled by qualified civilians.

Air Force Airlift and Refueling Units

Also warranting consideration is the possibility of transferring to civil-ian operation part of the airlift and air refueling missions now carried out

13. Logistics Management Institute, "Transfer of Destroyer Tenders and Repair Ships to the Military Sealift Command," LMI Task 76-11 (November 1976; pro-cessed), p. 21.

14. Ibid., pp. 14–15. One-time costs could be avoided if decisions to use MSC were made during the design and construction phase of new ships.

15. Sidney W. Emery, Jr., "Civilian-Manned Support Ships: A View from the Fleet," *U.S. Naval Institute Proceedings,* vol. 103 (April 1977), p. 38.

16. Ibid., p. 39.

by the U.S. Air Force. Any objections by the military establishment are likely to focus on the dangers of relying on civilian personnel. But such objections fly in the face of existing national policy that leans heavily on the use of the Civil Reserve Air Fleet (CRAF) in mobilization planning. The CRAF policy gives authority to the President to mobilize elements of U.S. commercial airlines during emergencies, ostensibly to airlift personnel and equipment worldwide.

The air refueling mission should likewise be examined. Refueling aircraft, now assigned to the Strategic Air Command, serve essentially the same purpose as the Navy oilers mentioned above. In any event, because of their vulnerability to enemy aircraft, Air Force tankers are designed to operate principally in areas in which the probability of contact with the enemy is small.

Army Support Units

Because of the nature of its operations, the Army appears to have fewer opportunities to employ civilians in units traditionally manned by soldiers. Apart from such questions as discipline and motivation, a large number of Army units, including some used in a supporting role, routinely operate close to the combat zone. There are also, however, support units operating almost exclusively in the rear areas that could be considered appropriate candidates for civilian substitution. In fact, over the past several years, in reaction to the Nunn amendment calling for improvements in the tooth-to-tail ratio in Europe,[17] the Army has begun to replace military personnel with foreign nationals in its Combat Equipment Group in Europe. This organization is responsible for storing, maintaining, and issuing the equipment kept at certain sites in Europe with which combat units based in the United States would be mated in wartime. A military cadre in the group would oversee the issue, and the deploying troops would activate the equipment. The civilians, of course, would not accompany the troops.[18]

Moreover, in 1975 the Army divulged plans to hire 3,800 foreign nationals to fill positions in finance, supply, administrative, maintenance,

17. 88 Stat. 401.

18. For a fuller discussion of this program, see "Continuing Problems with U.S. Military Equipment Pre-positioned in Europe," Report to the Joint Economic Committee by the Comptroller General of the United States (July 27, 1976; processed).

medical, engineering, and community support units in Europe.[19] How much further the Army can go in this direction is difficult to predict. But these examples suggest the type of units that deserve consideration.

AN ASSESSMENT of the policies that now limit the number of civilian employees indicates that, even within present guidelines and without departing from traditional practices, the Department of Defense uses more uniformed employees than necessary. Moreover, if the nation is willing to break with the past and to contemplate using civilians in units and under conditions that have traditionally been considered the military's exclusive preserve, the potential for substituting civilian for military personnel is even greater.

The above examples indicate the kinds of changes that would be necessary to bring about more than a modest substitution of civilian for military personnel. In each case, the billets involved are those that are either routinely deployed or that would be deployed in an emergency; this would alter rotation requirements and hence make it possible to substitute civilians for still more positions. The measures discussed represent major breaks with tradition, but they should not be dismissed out of hand. Since most of these billets would be in the blue-collar category, the analysis indicates that substitution would not be profitable at current compensation levels. However, if the relative costs of military and blue-collar civilians, which now favor the former, flip-flop in the future—as a result of blue-collar pay reform or of increases in military recruitment incentives—the options will become attractive.

19. *Fiscal Year 1976 and July-September 1976 Transition Period Authorization for Military Procurement, Research and Development, and Active Duty, Selected Reserve, and Civilian Personnel Strengths,* Hearings before the Senate Committee on Armed Services, 94:1 (Government Printing Office, 1975), pt. 3, p. 1197.

CHAPTER SIX

GOVERNMENT OR PRIVATE ENTERPRISE?

Apart from the question of whether to use military or federal civilian employees in a range of jobs is the issue of whether the work should be done by government or private-sector employees in the first place.

Relative Costs of In-House and Private Contractor Operations

The discussion thus far has centered on the relative costs of manning billets in defense organizations. It is equally important to compare the costs of having a job done by defense employees with those of having it done by a private contractor.

As discussed in chapter 2, apart from military "essentiality," disruptions or slowdowns of defense programs, and the like, relative cost is supposed to be the determining factor in selecting between in-house and private sources for commercial and industrial activities. Procedures to be followed by the military services in preparing comparative cost analyses are set forth in Department of Defense directives. Far more than manpower costs are involved. Shown below are the cost elements that must be estimated:[1]

For contract operations:
Contract cost (price paid to supplier)
Transportation charges not included in contract price
Contract administration
Government-furnished materials and supplies
Contractor use of government-owned equipment and facilities

1. For a detailed description of these cost elements, see Department of Defense, Instruction 4100.33, "Operation of Commercial or Industrial Activities," Enclosure 3, July 16, 1971.

Rehabilitation, modification, or expansion of government-owned
equipment and facilities

Incentive or premium costs

Standby maintenance cost

Other costs (for example, severance pay for federal civilians resulting
from the shutdown of an in-house activity).

For in-house operations:

Military personnel services

Civilian personnel services

Other personnel costs (for example, travel and per diem allowances)

Materials, supplies, utilities, and other services

Overhead costs

Federal taxes (which would be received if the work were done under
contract)

Depreciation

Opportunity cost (the money forgone by operating government equipment and facilities)

Interest (estimate of interest government would have to pay to borrow
for capital investment)

Insurance (property and employee liability)

Other indirect costs (central administrative services).

For the most part, cost studies made under these ground rules have
been considered unreliable and have become controversial. Characteris-
tically, the adversaries are the labor unions, represented by the American
Federation of Government Employees of the AFL-CIO, and U.S. business interests, represented by industrial lobbyists. For example, citing the
"failure of decisionmakers to determine the true costs of contracting-out,"
the AFGE president contended that it is rarely true that it is cheaper to
contract out than to perform a given service in-house.[2]

In addition to the obvious complexities involved in calculating relative
costs (how are opportunity costs to be imputed?), two major points of
contention have been emphasized.

First, the accuracy of contract estimates has been questioned, more so
with respect to procedures used by the Army and Navy than those used
by the Air Force. Until recently, the Air Force was the only service that
used *firm* bids from prospective contractors in its cost studies; in the

2. "Statement of Kenneth T. Blaylock, National President, American Federation
of Government Employees, before the Subcommittee on Manpower and Personnel
of the Senate Armed Services Committee," July 12, 1977, pp. 3, 4 ff.

Army and the Navy, the in-house personnel prepared the estimates for both in-house and contract operation. Thus the government employees making the Army and Navy estimates had to know a potential contractor's method of management and operation and cost structure. This generally meant assuming that a contractor would do a job in the same way as it would be done in-house, with the same organizational structure and a similar number of people. The comparison then rested on relative pay and benefits of government and private-sector employees and biased the results in favor of in-house operations, since contractors generally employ fewer personnel than the government to accomplish a given job. These differences in procedure at least partly explain the marked disparity in the results of cost comparisons conducted during fiscal years 1973 through 1975:[3]

Service	Total number of cost comparisons	Comparisons favoring contract bids	
		Number	Percentage
Army	69	33	47.8
Navy	47	6	12.8
Air Force	79	70	88.6

In assessing the services' determination of contract costs, the General Accounting Office identified three problems: (1) apparent overstatement of costs "to justify continuance of in-house performance"; (2) unsupported assumptions made in estimating costs; and (3) unreliable cost estimates obtained from informational quotations.[4] In August 1976, the Army and Navy were directed to adopt the Air Force practice of making cost comparisons on the basis of firm bids. It is too early to judge the effects of that change.

Another problem is that in-house costs are sometimes understated because the full cost of accruing pension benefits for federal civilian employees is not included. The magnitude of the problem and its effects on contract decisions are far from clear. One General Accounting Office report suggests that the change might have less effect than expected. It applied revised cost factors to thirty-nine studies that had previously used the 7 percent retirement accrual cost. After correcting for the higher

3. Norman E. Betaque, Jr., and Thomas M. O'Hern, Jr., "Contracting for Services in the Department of Defense," in Defense Manpower Commission, *Defense Manpower Commission Staff Studies,* vol. 2 (Government Printing Office, 1976), p. 24.
4. General Accounting Office, *How to Improve Procedures for Deciding between Contractor and In-house Military Base Support Services* (GAO, 1977), p. 10.

retirement accrual rate, the GAO found that "the adjusted in-house costs would not have reversed any of the services' decisions to either continue in-house performance or to contract the activities."[5]

In response to such criticisms, the Carter administration attempted to resolve some of the difficulties. After conducting a comprehensive study of policies concerning government reliance on private enterprise, the Office of Federal Procurement Policy proposed a number of changes in the methods of making cost comparisons. The proposals included such things as (1) developing a detailed cost handbook, (2) accounting more completely for indirect costs, (3) basing all cost comparisons on a competitive firm bid or proposal from industry, and (4) prescribing standard cost factors.[6] As of May 1978, the revisions were still under review, with publication of revised directives expected in early fiscal 1979.

A related point is important. It is possible that a military service that converts an in-house activity to a lower-cost private operation would have to face a higher budget than if the operation had been retained by government employees. This seeming paradox arises because some of the cost elements of in-house operations are not accounted for in the individual budgets of the military services (for example, the cost of military retirement and the difference between the government's 7 percent contribution and the actual cost of federal civilian retirement). Thus, in changing over to a private operation, a service's published budget is increased by most of the total contract cost, but is decreased only by the portion of the in-house costs that were initially charged to it. Though a net saving accrues to the taxpayer, the prospect of defending what appears to be a larger budget in Congress is hardly an incentive for the military services to pursue the contract option, although it may be cheaper.

Even if these problems were resolved, it would be risky to generalize about the relative cost of in-house and contracted operations. As the description of the cost elements indicates, more is involved than comparing manpower costs. The composition of the in-house work force, the geographical area affected, relative amounts of capital and labor, relative productivity of respective labor forces, and the like would have to be taken into consideration.

Nonetheless, some insight into relative costs can be obtained by examining previous conversions. The classical example of the potential bene-

5. Ibid., p. 9.

6. *Federal Register,* November 21, 1977, pp. 59814–15.

fits of contract operation is the Reese-Vance comparison conducted by the Rand Corporation in 1974.[7]

Reese Air Force Base and Vance Air Force Base have the same mission—undergraduate pilot training. They train approximately the same number of pilots each year, and their aircraft inventories, flying program, plant capacity, and geographical areas are similar. Reese Air Force Base is operated by Air Force military and civilian manpower, while many support services at Vance are provided by a private contractor.

The Rand analysis concluded that Vance was the more efficient base. In providing approximately the same output (trained pilots), Vance used 29 percent fewer personnel and 15 percent fewer dollars.[8] The average cost per man-year at Vance was higher than at Reese, but because Vance used fewer people that difference was offset. The need for fewer people at Vance has been attributed to more efficient management by private organizations. Particular note was taken of "the fewer number of suborganizations and supervisors used at Vance than at Reese, which is compelled to use the standard Air Force organizational structure."[9]

This example emphasizes that comparison of in-house versus contractor costs is sensitive to the scope of operations. For example, under single-function contracting, in which individual services are obtained from separate and generally small contractors, the cost of the operation when performed in-house is not likely to include any overhead allocation since the individual function constitutes only a small portion of the workload. Under a multifunction or "umbrella" approach, however, a single contractor is retained to perform a wide range of base operations or support functions. In this case, the workload is large enough to permit the con-

7. Robert M. Paulson and Arnold Zimmer, *An Analysis of Methods of Base Support: Contractor Operations versus Standard Operations at Two Undergraduate Pilot Training Bases* (Rand Corporation, March 1975). As this report contains privileged contractor information, its use is restricted. However, it is summarized in Marvin M. Gordon and John D. Sitterson, Jr., "The Support Forces," in Defense Manpower Commission, *Defense Manpower Commission Staff Studies*, vol. 2 (GPO, 1976).

8. Paulson and Zimmer, *An Analysis of Methods of Base Support*, p. vi. It should be noted that only out-of-pocket costs were considered; some important elements, such as retirement and training costs, were omitted. Generally, these omissions cause the difference in the cost of the two operations to be understated.

9. Gordon and Sitterson, "The Support Forces," p. 24. According to the Paulson and Zimmer study, one of the key findings—in addition to the potential for economies from relying on private enterprise—was that the military services could expect to achieve savings in base operating support by revising their management techniques even without contracting them out.

tractor to assume some middle- and upper-management responsibilities and positions, enabling a larger proportion of overhead costs to be imputed to in-house operations in the comparison.[10]

An analysis of conversions from in-house work to contracts during fiscal 1974 indicate some of the budgetary advantages. The results are summarized below:[11]

Activity	*Number of conversions*	*Average percentage savings*
Laundry and dry cleaning	3	39
Custodial services	25	39
Refuse collection and disposal	4	47
Food services	5	22

Although the differences can be accounted for partly by higher government wages, differences in manning standards as described in the Vance-Reese example must be considered.

The above analysis indicates that the private sector can provide certain services to the armed forces more efficiently than they can be provided by government organizations staffed by either federal civilian or military employees. Thus, whether the Department of Defense has adequately exploited the use of private enterprise, an issue with important budgetary implications, deserves closer examination.

Further Opportunities

In fiscal 1975, defense commercial and industrial activities accounted for about 465,000 man-years of labor, of which 96,000, or about 21 percent, were expended under contract.[12] The remaining 79 percent was justified for in-house operation for the reasons shown in table 6-1. Cost was the criterion in justifying only about 11 percent of the man-years involved.

Implementation of the ground rules governing contract activities has been criticized on several counts by the General Accounting Office. In its

10. See Betaque and O'Hern, "Contracting for Services in the Department of Defense," pp. 31–38.

11. Gordon and Sitterson, "The Support Forces," p. 22.

12. It has been estimated that an additional 30,000 man-years were contracted but not reported. See Department of Defense, "National Defense Budget Estimates for FY 1979" (1978; processed), p. 104.

Table 6-1. Number of Man-Years Spent on Commercial and Industrial Activities by
In-House and Contract Personnel, Department of Defense, Fiscal Year 1975

Justification for in-house and contract operation	*Man-years (thousands)*	*Percentage of total man-years*
In-house activities	**368.4**	**79.3**
Less disruption and delay	109.5	23.6
Military essentiality	162.0	34.9
No alternative source	27.8	6.0
Less costly	16.9	3.6
No reason given	52.2	11.2
Contracted activities	**96.1**	**20.7**
Less costly	33.9	7.3
Unrelated to cost	45.5	9.8
No reason given	16.7	3.6
Total	**464.6**	**100.0**

Source: Office of the Assistant Secretary of Defense (Manpower and Reserve Affairs), "An Overview of Contract Services in the Department of Defense" (October 1976; processed), p. 15. Figures are rounded.

analysis, the GAO found that of the $2 billion spent in fiscal 1975 to provide base support services (transportation, food, custodial services, minor construction, and the like), about three-fourths were allocated to in-house operations.[13] The GAO concluded that inventories of Department of Defense commercial and industrial operations were unreliable partly because of "inappropriate justifications given for continuing in-house performance."[14] Moreover, many activities have been inappropriately excluded from consideration; for example, those involved with routine maintenance and repair, and food, bus, and custodial services have not been reviewed. Twenty-two of twenty-seven GAO studies of such activities concluded that contractors would be less costly and that the savings would be $3.7 million.[15]

The potential for transferring additional in-house functions to private contractors is difficult to estimate. A rough indication is provided by examining the proportion of each activity that is not now using contract manpower, as shown by service in table 6-2. Differences among the services in the use of contract manpower are conspicuous. For example, about one-third of the Navy and one-half of the Army laundry and dry

13. Comptroller General of the United States, *How to Improve Procedures for Deciding between Contractor and In-House Military Base Support Services* (General Accounting Office, 1977), p. 1.

14. Ibid., p. ii.

15. Ibid., pp. 19–20. According to the GAO, the savings are understated because the cost of federal civilian employee benefits are understated.

Table 6-2. In-House Commercial and Industrial Activities, by Service, Fiscal Year 1975[a]

Type of activity	Total number of separate operations			Number of operations performed in-house as a percentage of total		
	Army	Air Force	Navy	Army	Air Force	Navy
Laundry and dry cleaning services	42	31	23	52	19	70
Custodial services	109	88	104	17	5	38
Refuse collection and disposal services	80	76	61	24	57	25
Food services	105	158	111	41	87	34
Office equipment	51	25	13	6	8	15
Motor vehicle maintenance	82	129	80	55	76	59
Guard services	60	108	108	70	100	81
Utility systems	442	633	401	30	86	61
Cataloging	9	5	5	89	40	80
Training and consultant services	46	27	25	11	100	56
Photographic, film, and television services	98	99	52	61	99	73
Administrative telephone services	92	90	66	66	100	21
Contractor engineering and technical services	3	...	7	0	...	0
Aircraft fueling service	15	83	36	87	100	33
Data processing service	122	98	115	36	93	31
Maintenance of data processing equipment	38	5	32	0	0	22
Systems design, development, and programming service	83	57	68	24	95	75
Repair of buildings and structures	65	114	82	9	26	21
Repair of surfaced areas	54	97	34	15	41	29

Source: Norman E. Betaque, Jr., and Thomas M. O'Hern, Jr., "Contracting for Services in the Department of Defense," in Defense Manpower Commission, *Defense Manpower Commission Staff Studies*, vol. 2 (GPO, 1976), p. 30.
a. Data shown are for fiscal 1975; a cursory inspection of fiscal 1976 data indicates little change.

cleaning facilities employ contract personnel, whereas about four-fifths of the Air Force facilities do. About 86 percent of Air Force utility systems are operated by defense manpower; the corresponding figures for the Army and the Navy are 30 percent and 61 percent. Though far from conclusive, these data imply that there are additional opportunities for contract operations.

There is also evidence to suggest that the military services could rely to a greater extent on private enterprise for aircraft depot maintenance.

According to Department of Defense policies, all of the aircraft depot maintenance workload not considered "mission essential" and at least 30 percent of the mission-essential workload should be performed to the maximum extent feasible by commercial sources.[16] Yet, according to the General Accounting Office, in fiscal 1975, a far smaller share of the aircraft workload was performed commercially. For example, the GAO indicated that the Navy was assigning about 78 percent of its mission-essential workload and about 65 percent of its workload not considered mission essential to its own facilities.[17] According to the GAO:

Despite the requirement stated in OMB Circular A-76, few formal cost comparisons were made in determining whether aircraft depot maintenance will be done organically or commercially.[18] The justification used for performing depot maintenance in-house is usually mission essentiality rather than relative cost.[19]

Indeed, the military services have tried to contract additional work. As discussed in chapter 3, however, Congress blocked those attempts in 1977. The administration appears ready to try again. For example, in its budget for fiscal 1979, the Air Force reduced by about 6,000 its manpower authorization in anticipation of converting that number of jobs to contract. The other services proposed smaller conversions. Whether or not Congress will go along with the proposals remains to be seen.[20]

THE POSSIBILITIES for substituting contract manpower for both military and civilian personnel have not been fully tapped and further opportunities should be explored.

The force of available—admittedly scanty—evidence indicates that where appropriate it would be cost-effective for the Pentagon to expand

16. Department of Defense, Directive 4151.1, "Use of Contractor and Government Resources for Maintenance of Matériel," June 20, 1970.

17. General Accounting Office, *Should Aircraft Depot Maintenance Be In-House or Contracted? Controls and Revised Criteria Needed* (GAO, 1976), p. 5.

18. Office of Management and Budget, "Policies for Acquiring Commercial or Industrial Products and Services for Government Use," Circular no. A-76, revised, October 18, 1976.

19. Ibid., p. 19.

20. Office of the Assistant Secretary of Defense (Public Affairs), "Air Force Announces Plan to Study Activities for Possible Private Contractor Conversion," News Release no. 134-78, March 14, 1978. Apparently shying away from umbrella contracts, the Air Force proposes to convert many relatively small activities located at forty-five locations. The largest single conversion proposed involves about 1,100 jobs at Edwards Air Force Base, California.

its association with private enterprise. The extent of that association and budgetary implications are difficult to pin down, but it is safe to say, based on relevant experience, that for each 10,000 man-years of activities contracted out under an umbrella arrangement, at least $30 million could be saved annually.[21]

21. This is a relatively conservative estimate. Another observer concludes that "the substitution of 250,000 contract hires for 250,000 direct hires could save about $1 billion a year." See Richard V. L. Cooper, *Military Manpower and the All-Volunteer Force* (Rand Corporation, September 1977), p. 301.

CHAPTER SEVEN

SHAPING THE DEFENSE CIVILIAN
WORK FORCE:
CONCLUSIONS AND RECOMMENDATIONS

A critical examination of the civilian component of the U.S. defense establishment is long overdue. Its size and composition have been dictated as much by political and institutional pressures as by the needs of national security. This combination of diverse interests has tended to discourage rational review. Recent developments, however, have increased the cost of inertia and should serve as an incentive for decisionmakers to scrutinize more closely the costs and benefits of change. First, if the United States is to remain apace of improvements in Soviet military capabilities without unnecessarily increasing the financial burden of defense, a more efficient defense establishment will be required. Second, the prospect that this nation will not be able to sustain an all-volunteer force of appropriate size and quality without incurring exorbitant costs makes the search for alternatives to military manpower all the more important.

Accordingly, in the analysis we have asked whether all the jobs that defense civilians are now doing need to be done and, if so, whether employing civilians is the most efficient way to get them done. But we have also asked whether the nation should rely to a greater extent on civilians, either in the government or the private sector, to do some of the jobs now being performed by military personnel.

The principal purpose has not been to estimate the magnitude of proposed changes, although where possible this has been attempted. Rather it is to provide the bases and rationale for such changes, to recommend a framework that would lead to the development of an appropriate balance of defense manpower resources, and to suggest topics needing further investigation and research.

General Conclusions

The analysis concludes that many defense civilian employees are paid in excess of an appropriate market wage, that many of the jobs now being done by defense civilians cannot be justified in national security terms, and that the components of the total defense work force—military, federal civilian, and contract employees—are not efficiently proportioned. By redressing imbalances in federal civilian compensation, by judiciously pruning the defense support establishment, by selectively converting military positions to civilian billets, and by increasing reliance on private enterprise, wherever appropriate, the nation could avoid paying more than is necessary to field its present military forces. More important is the prospect that large increases in the defense payroll to maintain desired standards among military recruits could be avoided, freeing resources that could be put to better use elsewhere in the defense establishment.

Compensation of Defense Civilian Employees

Many defense civilian employees are being compensated at unjustifiably high levels. First, a relatively large unexplained increase in average grades in the white-collar ranks has occurred between 1975 and 1978. Second, and more obvious, quirks in the formula now used to calculate pay increases for federal blue-collar workers have caused the pay of many of these workers to exceed the levels required to maintain comparability with their counterparts in private industry. Measures to correct both problems would yield savings of over $900 million a year when fully implemented.

Utilization of Defense Civilians

The Department of Defense presently employs more labor than can be justified by national security requirements. The military base structure and the defense logistics establishment, which together employ two-thirds of all defense civilians, are among the major reasons for this and need to be reassessed.

NUMBER OF BASES. By most accounts, the military services, bowing to political pressures, maintain more bases than they think are necessary for national security. The development of a base structure adapted to military requirements would lead to savings but, unless the missions performed at the bases that were closed down were also eliminated, such savings would probably be modest.

EFFICIENCY OF BASES. Larger savings could be expected if bases were operated more efficiently. Comparisons of quasi-commercial and industrial services produced by government organizations with similar services obtained through private contractors reveal that in-house operations are more labor-intensive than necessary. Adoption of private enterprise management and manning criteria could yield substantial savings in manpower devoted to base operations support.

LOGISTICS. The appropriate size of the defense logistics establishment and the efficiency with which it operates have long been subjects of considerable debate, intensified recently by concern over the state of readiness of U.S. combat forces. As matters stand, little is known about the relation between the frequency of major equipment maintenance, its duration, and the effectiveness of the overall force. Moreover, whether or not redundancies exist in the worldwide network of supply installations, some of which are operated by the military services and some by the centralized Defense Logistics Agency, is unclear. The Pentagon has undertaken programs to promote efficiency in the logistics establishment that promise eventual savings of about $2 billion a year. To the extent that the military services can implement the improvements more widely and at an accelerated pace, the savings could be realized sooner and could be larger.

The Defense Manpower Mix

We conclude that the present mix of manpower employed by the Department of Defense—about 2 million military, some 1 million federal civilians, and an estimated 130,000 private-sector civilians—is not now cost-effective and, if present trends continue, is likely to become less so.

CIVILIAN SUBSTITUTION. Our analysis shows that for certain positions federal civilian employees could be substituted for military personnel without jeopardizing national security. The Department of Defense now assigns armed forces personnel to jobs that do not strictly require military incumbents. After accounting for all billets which, by conservative reckoning, would call for military personnel—those deployed overseas, those that would be deployed abroad in a contingency, and those needed for rotation purposes—about 377,000 billets now occupied by the military could be considered candidates for civilian substitution. The exact number that could be filled by qualified civilians without risk to national security would have to be determined in more detailed analyses. To go beyond that potential, the possibilities of using civilians in units and under conditions that traditionally have been considered the military's exclusive domain (for example, naval fleet support) should be probed.

Whether or not substitutions should be effected also depends on costs. In present circumstances, the total cost of filling a white-collar job with a federal civilian is 20 to 25 percent less, on average, than filling the same job with an equivalent military employee. In the case of a blue-collar job, the reverse is true. As prospects for maintaining appropriate quality of military recruits diminish in the face of demographic and economic trends, it is likely that military pay will increase more rapidly than federal civilian pay. If this occurs, the financial advantage of replacing military personnel with white-collar civilians would grow larger and it may even become profitable to consider blue-collar substitution, particularly if legislation is enacted to correct the anomalies in the blue-collar wage-setting process discussed in chapter 2.

RELIANCE ON THE PRIVATE SECTOR. All available evidence indicates that a wide range of goods and services now being provided by government employees can just as well be delivered by private enterprise. At last count, of a total of some 500,000 man-years expended in these so-called commercial and industrial activities, all but 130,000 involved defense employees. How many of the other 370,000 man-years of defense effort could be transferred to private contractors is difficult to estimate, but the evidence indicates that opportunities exist in both base operations and depot maintenance activities. Although the cost advantages are difficult to determine precisely, by most counts they are significant, averaging 15 to 20 percent. Savings are particularly apparent when a single contractor is retained under an umbrella contract to perform a wide range of base operating and support activities.

Encouraging Reform

It is impossible to predict with precision the extent to which base and logistics activities can be reduced and the extent to which the composition of the defense labor force can and should be shifted without undue risk to national security. That task requires detailed analysis that should be accomplished within the Department of Defense.

Three factors are critical to a revision of current practices to encourage the Department of Defense to seek a more efficient allocation of its manpower. First, national policy with respect to the composition of the defense labor force, now obscured in a thicket of complexity and misunderstanding, should be reassessed and made more explicit. Second, constraints now imposed on the Pentagon by the White House and Congress, which contribute to inefficiencies in the composition of the defense labor force, need to be reexamined in view of the nation's security requirements and economic prospects. And third, disincentives inherent in the Pentagon's planning, programming, and budgeting process, which now discourage military managers from seeking a more efficient allocation of manpower, should be removed.

Composition of the Defense Labor Force

The general rules underlying the present composition of the defense work force have evolved over the years in piecemeal fashion. In essence, they state that uniformed personnel are to be assigned to jobs that, according to the armed forces, require a military incumbent. Civilians should fill all other positions. The services have to prove not only that military personnel are required, but that a "compelling" reason exists for not using private contractors rather than federal civilian employees.

As discussed in chapter 3, these guidelines have not been taken seriously by many of the participants in the decision process. Military managers enjoy wide leeway in defining jobs "requiring" a uniformed incumbent and there is little evidence that civilian policymakers scrutinize these decisions. Moreover, it can be argued that a policy prescribing the use of civilians when military personnel are not required, without considering budgetary implications, may now be inappropriate.[1]

Accordingly, the following steps should be taken:

1. A clear distinction must be drawn between jobs that, for reasons of national security, should be filled by military employees and those that can be filled by civilians. The services should develop more precise criteria for military incumbency and a clearer rationale for reserving additional billets for military personnel that otherwise might not require a uniformed employee. The staffs of both the Office of the Secretary of Defense and the Office of Management and Budget should review in

---

1. Such a policy was more appropriate to a conscription system. National decisionmakers wanted as few people in uniform as possible, largely because of the social and political costs of coercion.

detail the job structure of each military service and defense agency, the deployability of defense billets, and the policies governing rotation, promotion, and career development of military employees.

2. The conditions under which a job has to be performed by government employees must be defined. The Department of Defense and the Office of Management and Budget should jointly develop more explicit rules governing the restriction of certain industrial and commercial activities to in-house operations.

3. All other positions should be filled by whichever type of manpower is most effective in relation to its cost. The Department of Defense should prepare comprehensive and detailed specifications for determining the full costs allocable to military and civilian employees for all positions not requiring military or in-house incumbents. The analysis presented in chapter 5 and appendix C provides a starting point; the remainder of the task can be completed only with access to detailed information of the kind most readily available within the Pentagon.

Political Constraints

The extent to which the Department of Defense can be expected to pursue greater efficiencies depends in large measure on the freedom with which the military services can control their resources. As matters stand, the services are sometimes compelled to maintain installations for which a military requirement does not exist, they must operate under separate and often inconsistent limitations on military and civilian employment levels imposed by Congress and the administration, and—most recently —the flexibility that used to stem from the option of obtaining some labor services through contracts with private industry has been sharply curtailed. In short, the combined effect of many constraints now imposes a drastically restricted range of solutions over which the Pentagon has little control.

RESTRICTIONS ON BASE CLOSURES. It would be naive to expect that the influence of political considerations can be eliminated, especially in the short run. The base closure issue constitutes a particularly refractory problem, whose solution depends on whether those concerned believe that the adverse economic impact of closing a base on its surrounding community can be offset. The Defense Manpower Commission concluded that it can be if base closings are approached as part of a long-range program, and if part of the savings from base closures are earmarked for economic assistance to the affected communities.[2] More specifically, the commission argued that plans for base realignments and closures be developed three years before implementation to allow time for local economic adjustment assistance progams to be worked out and for employees whose positions are eliminated to find new jobs. Even then, *"communities still might not like the planned closures or realignments; but their elected representatives, having something to give in return, would be enabled to take a more positive attitude toward the closing as an improvement in the national interest."*[3] For this proposal to work—and it deserves serious consideration—short-run costs might have to be accepted to achieve long-run savings.

CEILING CONTROLS. As discussed in chapter 3, the White House and Congress impose ceilings on defense civilian employment. As long as national policymakers maintain their interest in controlling the growth of the federal civilian work force independently of workload, defense planners will have no incentive to consider the trade-offs among military personnel, civilian employees, and contract operations that are vital to promoting a more efficient defense establishment. Since ceiling controls are symbols of that interest, their removal might make Pentagon officials more confident that civilian substitution, to the extent warranted by cost and effectiveness, would be accepted by the administration and Congress. Many of the latter might still be concerned that a removal of ceilings would invite inefficiency in the military establishment. It should be pointed out, however, that there is another, and in many respects superior, way to improve efficiency.

As matters stand, attention during the defense budget review focuses on resources (military personnel, procurement, operations and maintenance, and the like) to operate the defense establishment. This is useful and necessary in making clear what is being bought, but not in clarifying what it is being used for. Attention ought to be directed toward defense "programs," or categories of military functions. These include both the mission functions assigned to the operating forces (strategic, tactical air, naval, and the like) and those assigned to support activities (for example, base operations, logistics, and training). These groups are not "outputs"

2. Defense Manpower Commission, *Defense Manpower: The Keystone of National Security* (Government Printing Office, April 1976), pp. 132–33.

3. Marvin N. Gordon and John D. Sitterson, Jr., "The Support Forces," in Defense Manpower Commission, *Defense Manpower Commission Staff Studies,* vol. 2 (GPO, 1976), p. 93 (emphasis in original).

in a strict sense, but nevertheless they merge into defense programs that in turn contribute to the various capabilities needed to protect U.S. national security.

With this approach, the armed services committees, instead of authorizing employment levels, would set funding ceilings for each "program." This would require, for example, review of the entire logistics establishment and explicit consideration of the trade-offs among military, civilian, and contract manpower options available to provide the necessary services. A funding ceiling on each program would leave the Department of Defense free to allocate resources within the program. Substantially the same purpose would be served if, as an alternative to funding ceilings, the armed services committees authorized specified military forces (numbers of divisions, ships, or air squadrons) and activity levels (numbers of aircraft flying hours, ship steaming hours, ship overhauls, students, or bases).

The shift in emphasis—from *resources needed* to *purposes served*—recommended here is likely to make the defense budget process more complicated than it is now, and it could require a rethinking of the respective roles of the budget, armed services, and appropriations committees. The disadvantages, however, do not outweigh the benefits of the shift as a way of promoting greater rationality and efficiency in the Pentagon's essential, complex, and costly operations.

CONSTRAINTS ON PRIVATE ENTERPRISE. Recent restrictions on contracting for certain commercial and industrial activities, discussed in chapter 3, unquestionably reflect local interests. It is no secret that the strong proponents of these restrictions, most notably members of the House Armed Services, Appropriations, and Post Office and Civil Service Committees, represent geographical areas with government installations whose constituents might be detrimentally affected by increased reliance on private enterprise. As discussed in chapter 6, contracting for certain services with the private sector has proved to be more efficient and the prospects for even greater economies appear bright. Thus the Pentagon's opportunities to pursue this option should not be circumscribed, except by the requirements of national security.

Of course, congressmen have to be responsive to the needs and interests of their constituencies. Still, there is a broader national interest in promoting efficiency in the Department of Defense. Thus it remains unclear whether Congress would continue to bow to local interests if it were convinced that changes in the size and composition of the defense labor force could either improve the nation's military capability without increasing defense spending or decrease costs without compromising capability.

Congress should not be expected to yield on any of the issues—base closures, ceilings, or contracting—until the Department of Defense has demonstrated that it will not abuse such greater freedom of action. This can be done in part by developing both a coherent set of criteria governing the composition of the defense work force and a comprehensive set of manpower policies. A reasonable first step would be the cost analysis suggested above. The Pentagon should also be prepared to rationalize its installation structure and maintenance programs and to relate spending on both to forces and their level of readiness. Moreover, the military services should make a good-faith effort to improve the operational efficiency of their bases rather than responding to economy moves by offering the alternatives of closure and realignment.

Bureaucratic Influences

The Department of Defense is in the best position to determine the most efficient composition of its work force. The recommendations outlined above, if adopted, would provide the Pentagon with a clearer set of ground rules and greater flexibility in making manpower decisions. But before it can move toward attaining the best possible balance of military, civilian, and contract labor, the department will have to counter the management and bureaucratic influences that now inhibit military planners from pursuing a more efficient manpower program. Chief among these influences are the restrictions, some more apparent than real, imposed on management by the civilian personnel system; the incentives to employ military rather than civilian personnel inherent in the present method of budgeting; and the "lower cost–higher budget" paradox associated with the contracting option.

PROBLEMS IN CIVILIAN PERSONNEL MANAGEMENT. It is unlikely that military managers will be influenced in their choice between military and civilian personnel by cost comparisons alone. The argument that it costs the nation less to fill a job with a civilian than with a military employee is likely to be met with the counterargument, outlined in chapter 3, that because of the greater management flexibility inherent in military personnel systems, uniformed employees can be used more effectively than civilians. Some of the problems of managing civilians perceived by military planners are real; others are only apparent. In either event, it is unlikely that alternatives to military manpower will receive serious consideration by the military services until these concerns are dispelled. The problem was analyzed by the staff of the Defense Manpower Commission in 1975. Three of the complaints commonly voiced by military managers were found to be based on incorrect perceptions:

1. The authority to transfer or reassign civilians was found to be less restricted than military managers contend. Apart from controls to prevent arbitrary or capricious actions, management enjoys wide leeway. Many of the problems stem from the manner in which authority is perceived and used rather than from constraints imposed by the civil service system.

2. Complaints about the inability to deal effectively with marginal employees are also ill founded. Current regulations appear to provide managers with adequate tools that are not being used consistently or effectively.

3. The implications of the relative immobility of the civilian work force have been overemphasized. Unlike the "closed" military system, of which job reassignments are an integral part, the civilian system is "open," and the possibility of entry at any level reduces the need for mobility. Where it is required, however, mobility has been established as a condition of employment, and employees have been required to sign an appropriate agreement.

On the other hand, three problems often cited by defense managers were found to have greater validity:

4. Reductions in force of civilian employees have an unusually disruptive effect on productivity largely because of regulations that give priority to seniority, veterans' preference, and the like rather than merit.

5. Present legislation and regulations governing the civilian retirement system present obstacles to effective management. Once federal civilian employees attain normal retirement eligibility at the age of fifty-five, management has no say in retirement decisions until the individuals reach the age of seventy.

6. Defense managers are hampered in their efforts to manage the work week effectively because of the excessively restrictive legislation governing hours and days of work for civilian employees.[4]

4. This discussion is based largely on Howard W. Goheen, "Limitations on Managers Brought About by Restrictions of the Federal Civil Service System," in Defense Manpower Commission, *Defense Manpower Commission Staff Studies,* vol. 4 (GPO, 1976), pt. N.

Thus the present aversion of military managers toward civilian employees should not be considered immutable. Although a complete turnaround should not be anticipated, unfounded concerns could be dispelled through a training program that would emphasize how to use existing policies and directives to best advantage. The remaining constraints pose difficult but not insurmountable problems; appropriate legislation could give managers greater flexibility to deal with retirement, work schedule, and reduction in force problems. If enacted, some of President Carter's proposals to reform the federal civil service system would go a long way toward resolving these issues.

ELIMINATING THE "FREE GOOD" ELEMENT IN MILITARY MANPOWER. The separate systems governing military and civilian personnel create problems with important implications at the base or activity level. As discussed in chapter 3, military personnel are managed and budgeted for centrally, whereas civilian employees are managed and budgeted for locally. Since civilians are paid out of operations and maintenance (O&M) funds, over which local commanders have control, each civilian hired means less money for other uses of O&M funds (for example, utilities, rent, and supplies). Military personnel, on the other hand, are "free" since they do not affect the local commander's budget. This bias against civilian employees can be eliminated by a change in the method of accounting by which military employees would be considered a budgetary cost at the local level. Several schemes for doing this have been advanced; one suggests that the local commander be granted an increment to his O&M budget for each military position that had been authorized but not filled.[5] Pushing this idea one step further, the possibility of redesigning service budgets to consolidate military and civilian components in a single account should be given consideration. Under such a scheme, military and civilian pay would become parts of a single budget, eliminating the current "free good" element in military manpower. A limited attempt (Project PRIME) at such an approach was made in the mid-1960s. It failed, apparently because managers were never given the flexibility to make the trade-offs in formulating their budgets that was implied by such accounting procedures.[6]

5. Stephen Enke and Others, *Innovations for Achieving an AVF,* General Electric TEMPO Study for the Office of the Assistant Secretary of Defense (Manpower and Reserve Affairs) (January 3, 1972; processed), p. 55.

6. For a description of Project PRIME, see Steven Lazarus, "Planning-Programming-Budgeting Systems and Project PRIME," *Defense Industry Bulletin,* vol. 3 (January 1967), pp. 1–4.

THE "LOWER-COST–HIGHER BUDGET" PARADOX. If the possibilities for increased reliance on private enterprise are to get the attention they deserve, steps will have to be taken to straighten out the accounting muddle. As matters stand, the more the services utilize even the most efficient private contractors, the larger their budgets could become. This happens because, when a particular job is done under private contract, the full costs are borne by the military service, whereas some of the costs of conducting the operation in-house are not included in the budget of the particular military service. Most prominent is the cost of federal retirement; only part of civilian retirement costs and none of the military are included in the service budgets.

The problem can be resolved by a relatively simple budgetary change that would account for the full accrual cost of military and civilian retirement. For the military, this would mean converting from the present system, in which current retirement expenditures are budgeted in a central Department of Defense account, to a system in which each service is charged with appropriate accrued liability determined by actuarial methods. For civilian personnel, this change would mean that each service and defense agency would be charged with the *full* accrued liability instead of the 7 percent now used. Since other cost elements are also involved, this alteration would not completely resolve the paradox, but removing the retirement cost discrepancy would be a major step in that direction.

THE MEASURES proposed above—developing clearer ground rules, moderating the influence of special interests, and removing institutional biases —are designed to create a decisionmaking environment that would encourage the participants in the process to pursue greater efficiency in the defense labor force.

Since these steps would require Congress to relinquish certain existing controls, real or apparent, and the military to depart from some deeply rooted traditions, the proposed reform will not be easy. The difficult questions involved will require study, negotiation, and compromise. In some instances, disadvantages will have to be accepted by some parties in order to achieve a substantial improvement in the U.S. defense program as a whole.

Realistically, these questions will not be settled overnight; hence, planning and development for their implementation should begin at once. And it is important that these procedural issues not stand in the way of redressing the current grade and pay imbalances among federal civilian employees. In this respect, the administration should take steps to reduce the steady enrichment in the white-collar grade structure that has occurred since 1975. And Congress should enact legislation along the lines proposed by the administration to correct the overpayment of federal blue-collar employees. Taken together, these two measures would yield savings in excess of $150 million in the first year, reaching over $900 million annually within five years.

This is a tall order, but the stakes are high. If reform is not undertaken, the nation will continue to spend more than is necessary for defense, and the opportunity costs associated with maintaining the status quo will grow ever larger as time passes. Reshaping the system along the lines recommended above can improve the outlook.

Composition of the Defense Civilian Work Force

Defense civilians are employed by each of the four military services and the fourteen defense agencies in which they perform specialized functions supporting the entire defense establishment.[1] In addition to this organizational association, civilians are identified with one of two categories related to whether or not they are hired directly by the U.S. government.

Direct hire employees are recruited, work for, and are paid by the U.S. government. There are both U.S. citizens and foreign nationals in this category. *Indirect hire* workers, on the other hand, are foreign nationals who technically work for the host government but are assigned to work with U.S. military forces under contracts or agreements with that government on a reimbursable-cost or other basis. Table A-1 shows a distribution of defense civilians by agency and hiring category in fiscal 1978.

Government civilian employees are also categorized by classes of occupation. *Classified* workers are grouped and identified in categories of jobs sufficiently homogeneous as to subject matter, level of difficulty and responsibility, and qualification requirements to warrant similar treatment in personnel policies and pay administration. They are often called white-collar workers because of the nature of the jobs involved; and, since they are paid under a general schedule, they are sometimes referred to as general schedule (GS) employees. This pay schedule, which is divided

1. These organizations are: Office of the Secretary of Defense, Organization of the Joint Chiefs of Staff, Office of Overseas Dependents Education, Defense Advanced Research Projects Agency, Defense Communications Agency, Defense Contract Audit Agency, Defense Civil Preparedness Agency, Defense Intelligence Agency, Defense Investigative Service, Defense Mapping Agency, Defense Nuclear Agency, Defense Logistics Agency, and the Uniformed Services University of the Health Sciences. The National Security Agency, in which civilians are also employed, is excluded from discussion in this study since its size and specific missions are not publicly divulged.

85

Table A-1. Comparison of Projected Civilian and Military Personnel Strength in the Department of Defense, End of Fiscal Year 1978

Thousands of employees

	Civilians				
Component	Direct hire	Indirect hire	Total	Military, total	Civilians and military, total
Army	315	58	373	774	1,147
Navy	290	8	298	532	830
Marine Corps	16	3	18	192	211
Air Force	238	15	253	571	824
Defense agencies[a]	77	2	79	7[b]	79[c]
Total	936	86	1,021	2,069	3,091

Source: Data provided by the Office of the Assistant Secretary of Defense (Comptroller), March 1978. Figures are rounded.

a. Excludes National Security Agency.

b. Includes military personnel assigned to defense agencies; for accounting purposes these are included in the figures for their parent service.

c. For defense agencies, "Civilians and military, total" includes civilians only.

into eighteen grades of "difficulty and responsibility" of work, is a nation-wide wage scale annually adjusted by the President under rules established by Congress.[2]

Direct hire workers who are not in occupations classified under the general schedule and who work in the blue-collar skills (trade, craft, or manual labor) are known as Wage Board employees. In contrast to GS employees, whose pay levels are uniform and based on grade and step, the pay of Wage Board workers is governed by a "prevailing rate" system: levels are set by periodic wage surveys in each local labor market as prescribed by the Civil Service Commission.[3]

Table A-2 indicates the projected number of civilians employed by the Department of Defense in fiscal 1978 classified by type of hire, pay system, and citizenship; table A-3 shows the geographical distribution of civilians in 1976, the latest year for which data are available. Direct hire foreign nationals are employed principally in Asia, with 65 percent of them concentrated in three countries (Philippines, Korea, and

2. A salary range compartmented into ten steps is provided for grades GS-1 through GS-15, nine steps for GS-16, five steps for GS-17, and one for the highest grade—GS-18.

3. Within the Wage Board system, there are three categories of employees: supervisors (WS), leaders (WL), and nonsupervisors (WG). In addition to general schedule and Wage Board pay plans, there are twelve miscellaneous pay plans covering Canal Zone employees, experts and consultants, and the like. Only about 2 percent of all defense civilians are covered by these miscellaneous plans.

Table A-2. Projected Distribution of Defense Civilians, End of Fiscal Year 1978
Thousands of employees

Category	Army	Navy	Marine Corps	Air Force	Defense agencies	Total
Direct hire	315.4	289.6	15.6	238.1	77.2	935.9
General schedule	205.4	151.6	8.7	139.0	64.6	569.3
Wage Board	95.3	123.8	6.9	92.0	11.9	329.9
Foreign nationals	14.7	14.2	...	7.1	0.7	36.7
Indirect hire						
Foreign nationals	57.7	8.2	2.7	15.1	1.8	85.5
Total	373.1	297.8	18.3	253.2	79.0	1,021.4

Source: Data provided by the Office of the Assistant Secretary of Defense (Comptroller), March 1978. Figures are rounded.

Table A-3. Civilian Employees by Type, by Geographical Region, December 1976
Thousands of employees

Geographical region	Type of employee			
		Foreign nationals		
	U.S. direct hire	Direct hire	Indirect hire	Total
U.S. territories and special locations	886.7	2.8	...	889.5
Western Europe and related areas	21.3	5.8	59.2	86.3
Africa, Near East, and South Asia	0.7	0.8	...	1.5
Western Pacific	6.3	28.5	23.4	58.2
Western Hemisphere	0.6	1.3	...	1.9
Other	0.1	0.1	0.1	0.3
Total	915.7	39.3	82.7	1,037.7

Source: Office of the Assistant Secretary of Defense (Comptroller), Directorate for Management Information Operations and Control, "Selected Manpower Statistics" (May 1977; processed), p. 81.

Thailand). Over 90 percent of the indirect hire foreign nationals, on the other hand, are concentrated in Germany and Japan (including the Okinawa prefecture). But the vast majority—about 85 percent—of all defense civilians are employed in the United States and its territories.

Civilian personnel are employed by a wide variety of military organizations, categorized into seven fairly homogeneous groups according to their principal activities: force and fleet, intelligence and communications, matériel, training and education, medical, headquarters, and miscellaneous administrative (finance and accounting, recruiting, and the like). The distribution of defense civilians by occupation and organizational affiliation is shown in table A-4. Several points are worth noting: over one-half

Table A-4. U.S. Direct Hire Civilian Employees by Major Occupational Group and by Functional Area, September 1977

Thousands of employees

Major occupational groups	Force and fleet	Intelligence and communications	Matériel	Training and education	Medical	Departmental headquarters	Administrative	Total
Scientists and engineers	2.3	4.0	50.2	1.2	0.5	1.2	10.5	69.9
Other professionals	3.8	2.1	7.1	3.1	5.6	1.6	9.1	32.4
Management and administration personnel	41.5	5.9	85.5	9.9	3.7	6.4	21.1	174.0
Technicians and subprofessionals	26.2	8.4	84.7	14.8	5.6	2.3	13.8	155.8
Clerical workers	29.1	7.2	58.0	16.6	5.6	5.9	18.4	140.8
Service workers	11.2	0.7	17.0	5.3	7.6	0.9	5.8	48.5
Craftsmen, mechanics, and production workers	53.6	3.0	141.7	12.2	1.0	0.9	5.4	217.8
Laborers and operators	20.3	2.8	59.1	9.7	3.1	1.5	8.4	104.9
Total	188.0	34.1	503.3	72.8	32.7	20.7	92.5	943.9

Source: Data provided by the Office of the Assistant Secretary of Defense (Manpower, Reserve Affairs, and Logistics), March 1978. Figures are rounded.

Table A-5. Distribution of Military Personnel and Equivalent Full-Time Federal Civilians in Enlisted-Level Positions, Department of Defense, September 1977

Thousands of employees

Occupational category	Military	Civilian			Total, Department of Defense	Civilians as percentage of total
		General schedule	Wage Board	Total		
Infantry, gun crew, seaman specialist, and installations security personnel	259.6	5.8	7.1	12.9	272.5	4.7
Electronic equipment repairmen	164.2	4.1	24.2	28.3	192.5	14.7
Communications and intelligence specialists	149.0	6.0	...	6.0	155.0	3.9
Medical and dental specialists	78.7	8.9	...	8.9	87.6	10.2
Other technical and allied specialists	36.7	39.6	0.4	40.0	76.7	52.2
Administrative specialists and clerks	265.7	286.2	...	286.2	551.9	51.9
Electrical and mechanical equipment repairmen	340.9	3.6	70.4	74.0	414.9	17.8
Craftsmen	71.9	2.4	142.4	144.8	216.7	66.8
Service and supply handlers	161.6	7.6	96.9	104.5	266.1	39.3
Total	1,528.3	364.2	341.4	705.6	2,233.9	31.6

Source: Based on data provided by the Office of the Assistant Secretary of Defense (Manpower, Reserve Affairs, and Logistics), March 1978. Figures are rounded.

of all civilians are employed by matériel commands; of those, over half are involved in white-collar tasks. The second largest employer of civilians is the force and fleet group, which is responsible for operational control and peacetime administration of active and reserve force components. These include, for example, U.S. Army in Europe, Strategic Air Command, and the Air National Guard. Here again, close to two-thirds of the civilian workers are white-collar employees. The largest concentration of white-collar employees in the force and fleet commands is found in management and administration.

Another perspective is provided in table A-5, in which civilian personnel are classified by occupation in the same manner as that used by the Department of Defense for military personnel. This table, which includes only enlisted-level occupations, shows that civilians constitute the majority of total manpower in three occupational groups: craftsmen, administrative specialists and clerks, and other technical and allied specialists. The small concentration of civilians in communications and intelligence and in medical and dental specialties is also evident. Military and civilian administrative specialists and clerks, taken together, constitute close to 25 percent of total manpower in enlisted-level jobs, which underscores the growing paperwork nature of the defense establishment.

How Decisions Are Made on Civilian Manpower

The formal submission of the defense budget to Congress each January is the culmination of a process that begins about twenty months earlier with an estimate by the Joint Chiefs of Staff and the military services of the strategy and forces needed to meet perceived threats. The planning portion of the process encompasses a ten-month period during which the Joint Chiefs of Staff, the services, and the Office of the Secretary of Defense (working with the Office of Management and Budget and the National Security Council) bring together, through a complex political and bureaucratic process, the forces that military planners consider necessary and the dollars that administration officials expect to be available. During this part of the process, attention is focused on the broad aspects of the defense program; little consideration is given to detailed resource issues.

Definition of Manpower Needs

The beginning of the programming phase, about ten or eleven months before the budget submission, is marked by the issuance by the secretary of defense of "planning guidance," which includes such things as the fiscal, force planning, and manpower ground rules under which the military services are to design their programs. Guidance on manpower, however, remains fairly general. Typically, the services would not be under either military or civilian manpower constraints at this point, except perhaps for limitations on the number of military officers of general or flag rank or on the number of high-level classified civilians, say, in grades GS-13 and above.

The Joint Chiefs respond with a memorandum detailing their views on the ability of the military services to meet national security requirements within the established constraints. Concurrently, the military services provide the secretary of defense with their individual views of what constitutes the best application of available resources; this is expressed in what are called "program objective memoranda" (POMs). In developing such a memorandum, it should be noted, the services also take into account the implications of decisions made in previous budget reviews or in previous congressional action. For example, a presidential budget decision in the previous year might have established long-term manpower limitations or Congress might have mandated in a previous authorization bill a constraint on spending in a particular function. At any rate, POMs constitute the first documents in which the services state their requirements for military and civilian manpower.

The POMs are reviewed by analysts within the Office of the Secretary of Defense, who prepare issue papers, including one on manpower, in which imbalances in the service proposals are identified and alternatives presented for resolution to the secretary of defense. It is during this phase of the process that *fundamental* priorities in the allocation of resources could be questioned. But the issues raised often concern questions about the rate of weapon system acquisition and force levels. Only rarely is the possibility of changes in the overall composition of the defense labor force debated. The secretary's decisions are incorporated in a series of "program decision memoranda" (PDMs), one for each major program category covering the next five-year period (for example, the manpower PDM sets military and civilian manpower levels for each mission and support category).

Budget Assessments

These documents are the basis for developing the budget. During the review of the service budgets, attention is focused mainly on examining proposed increases in the previous year's spending level. Individual programs are reviewed jointly by budget examiners representing the Department of Defense and the Office of Management and Budget. A series of program budget decisions is made by the secretary of defense on various elements of the defense program, and when these decisions are combined they constitute the defense budget as submitted to the President.

The point at which the White House gets involved in the process has varied from time to time, depending on presidential management styles and special circumstances. Sometimes presidential consideration of fiscal or employment levels has preceded or has been concurrent with the joint budget review. At other times, presidents have become involved only after the joint review has been completed.

In any event, after presidential approval, the Office of Management and Budget issues a budget allowance letter, which establishes ceilings on dollars and civilian employment. Two separate ceilings on civilian manpower are imposed: one for employment in full-time direct hire permanent positions and another for total direct hire employment (which includes temporary, part-time, and intermittent employment).

Congressional Review

The defense budget is then submitted to Congress, where it runs a gauntlet of committees. The role of the budget committees is still evolving, and the level of detail with which they will review the defense budget is not precisely known. Budget committee hearings have been held, however, on the manpower components of the defense budget and the committees have made recommendations concerning the overall cost of defense manpower. For example, the House Budget Committee recommended a reduction of about 1.5 percent, or $750 million, in "personnel" costs for fiscal 1978.[1] Such recommendations express a particular concern of the committee but are not legislatively binding.

The influence of the armed services committees on defense manpower requirements and policies is more direct. These committees, which for many years have had the responsibility for authorizing active-duty and reserve military strength levels, have also, since fiscal 1975, set ceilings on civilian strengths.[2] Unlike the ceilings imposed by the Office of Man-

1. *First Concurrent Resolution on the Budget—Fiscal Year 1978,* Report of the House Committee on the Budget, Rept. No. 95-189, 95:1 (Government Printing Office, 1977), p. 27.

2. Apparently, questions of overlapping jurisdiction remain between some congressional committees. See, for example, the communications between the chairmen of the House Armed Services Committee and the House Post Office and Civil Service Committee in *Authorizing Appropriations, Fiscal Year 1978, for Military Procurement, Research and Development, and Civil Defense; and Prescribing Strengths for Active-Duty and Reserve Military Components and Civilian Personnel of the Defense Establishment, and Military Training Student Loads; and for Other Purposes,* House Committee on Armed Services, Rept. 95-194, 95:1 (GPO, 1977), pp. 102–3.

agement and Budget, these limitations apply to both direct and indirect hire civilians. Moreover, the secretary of defense is permitted to exceed the authorized ceiling if he considers it necessary in the national interest. In fiscal 1978, Congress provided a leeway of 1.25 percent.

Exempted from all ceilings imposed by the armed services committees and the Office of Management and Budget are: (1) employees performing civilian functions administered by the Department of Defense (for example, Corps of Engineers Civil Works); (2) employees in special programs for students and disadvantaged youth; (3) employees of the National Security Agency; and (4) employees paid from nonappropriated funds (for example, service club and exchange workers). When the total authorized is smaller than the number requested by the administration, reductions are often general, although specific areas, such as training or headquarters, might be identified as being of particular concern.

The appropriations committees not only review the defense budget from a different perspective—by appropriation category—but they generally get involved in greater detail. These committees, viewing the level of civilian manpower specified in the authorization bill as a maximum, more often than not specify reductions in that level and reduce the appropriation accordingly. Moreover, the appropriations committees are apt to identify reductions more specifically, sometimes by military unit.

It should be noted, however, that the military services enjoy some latitude to transfer funds within an appropriation category. This means that, in normal circumstances, a local manager has the choice of hiring a federal civilian employee or a private contractor, as long as the limits on total civilian employment imposed by the administration or Congress, and then parceled out by major military commands, are not exceeded. This would seem to provide managers with sufficient leeway, but the imposition of ceilings has been scored by the Department of Defense and the General Accounting Office as being unduly restrictive and inefficient.[3]

Criticism by both organizations centered on the inability of the military services to adjust employment levels with changes in workload, particu-

3. See, for example, the statement by Vice Admiral David H. Bagley, chief of naval personnel, in *Fiscal Year 1976 and July-September 1976 Transition Period Authorization for Military Procurement, Research and Development, and Active Duty, Selected Reserve, and Civilian Personnel Strengths*, Senate Armed Services Committee, 94:1 (GPO, 1975), pp. 1271–2, and Comptroller General of the United States, *Personnel Ceilings—A Barrier to Effective Manpower Management* (General Accounting Office, 1977).

larly in shipyards and depots. The seriousness of these problems and the extent to which they were caused by ceilings rather than by financial limitations or internal management difficulties is far from evident. The military services have been restricted, however, by new limitations (discussed in chapter 3) on contracting for commercial and industrial activities imposed by Congress in 1977.

Cost Derivations

This appendix sets forth the principal definitions and methodology underlying the cost estimates presented in chapter 4. The methodology is based largely on a 1977 Department of Defense study, "Average Cost of Military and Civilian Manpower in the Department of Defense."[1] Except where otherwise indicated, the estimates are based on unpublished data obtained from the Department of Defense. It is important to note that wide variations exist among the military services on some cost elements; the figures used here represent defense-wide averages. All costs are estimated 1978 dollars.

Cost Calculations

The full costs of military and defense civilian employees were developed from an examination of three types of costs: (1) compensation-related, (2) pipeline, and (3) support. Those related to compensation are shown in tables C-1 to C-5, pipeline costs are given in tables C-6 to C-8, support costs in table C-9, and average total costs in table C-10.

Compensation-related Costs

This category includes cost elements that are either directly paid to the employee or constitute a compensation-related benefit. For military employees, these are what have been called "regular military compensation," which includes basic pay and quarters and subsistence allowances; the tax advantage accruing because allowances are not taxable; and the

1. Office of the Assistant Secretary of Defense (Comptroller) (December 1977; processed).

Table C-1. Estimated Average Annual Compensation-related Costs, Military Personnel, by Grade, 1978

Costs in 1978 dollars

Grade	Annual standard composite less adjustments	Income tax adjust- ment	Basic allowance for quarters	Retirement benefits	Miscel- laneous[a]	Total com- pensation- related costs
Officer						
O-10	55,100	4,800	4,800	16,900	1,800	83,400
O-9	48,100	4,600	4,800	16,100	2,200	75,900
O-8	43,600	4,400	4,800	14,300	2,300	69,400
O-7	37,200	3,600	4,500	12,600	2,200	60,100
O-6	32,000	2,700	4,100	10,500	2,300	51,600
O-5	25,700	1,800	3,800	8,500	2,100	41,800
O-4	20,700	1,400	3,400	6,900	1,700	34,100
O-3	18,100	1,100	3,000	5,800	1,400	29,400
O-2	14,400	800	2,500	4,600	1,200	23,500
O-1	10,300	600	1,900	3,300	1,000	17,100
Warrant officer						
W-4	20,400	1,400	3,300	6,700	2,200	34,000
W-3	16,900	1,000	2,900	5,400	2,000	28,200
W-2	13,900	700	2,600	4,700	2,100	24,000
W-1	12,100	700	2,400	4,100	1,500	20,800
Enlisted						
E-9	17,700	1,000	2,800	5,500	2,400	29,400
E-8	15,100	800	2,600	4,700	2,400	25,600
E-7	12,700	700	2,400	4,000	2,300	22,100
E-6	10,700	700	2,200	3,300	2,000	18,900
E-5	8,800	700	1,900	2,700	1,700	15,800
E-4	7,600	600	1,500	2,400	1,600	13,700
E-3	6,900	500	1,300	2,000	1,400	12,100
E-2	6,400	400	1,100	1,800	1,400	11,100

Source: Office of the Assistant Secretary of Defense (Comptroller), "Average Cost of Military and Civilian Manpower in the Department of Defense" (December 1977; processed), adjusted and updated to reflect current compensation rates. Figures are rounded.

a. Includes variable medical costs (hospital operations plus Civilian Health and Medical Program of the Uniformed Services), unemployment compensation, dependency and indemnity compensation, and military educational benefits.

estimated costs of military retirement, reenlistment bonuses, dependents' indemnity compensation, medical and educational benefits, and unemployment compensation. For civilian employees, compensation includes base pay, overtime and holiday pay, life insurance, retirement and health benefits, unemployment and workmen's compensation, and terminal leave. Estimates of average costs by grade are shown in tables C-1

Table C-2. Estimated Average Annual Compensation-related Costs, General Schedule Civilians, by Grade, 1978

Costs in 1978 dollars

Grade	Base pay	Overtime and holiday	Life insurance	Retirement	Miscel-laneous[a]	Total compensation-related costs
18	47,500	...	200	9,700	900	58,300
17	47,500	...	200	9,700	900	58,300
16	47,500	...	200	9,700	900	58,300
15	42,100	...	200	8,700	800	51,800
14	35,800	...	200	7,300	800	44,100
13	30,300	400	100	6,200	800	37,800
12	25,100	400	100	5,100	700	31,400
11	20,800	300	100	4,200	700	26,100
10	19,500	300	100	4,000	700	24,600
9	17,000	300	50	3,400	700	21,500
8	16,000	300	50	3,300	700	20,350
7	14,100	250	50	2,800	700	17,900
6	13,000	200	50	2,700	700	16,600
5	11,500	200	50	2,300	800	14,800
4	10,100	200	50	2,000	900	13,300
3	8,600	150	50	1,800	1,000	11,600
2	7,400	100	50	1,200	1,400	10,200
1	6,300	100	50	1,200	1,700	9,400

Source: Same as table C-1.

a. Includes health benefits, unemployment compensation, workmen's compensation, and terminal leave.

through C-5. The derivation of the data in each column is described below for military and civilian personnel.

MILITARY PERSONNEL (TABLE C-1). The elements constituting total compensation-related costs of military personnel were calculated as follows:

Annual standard composite rates are average rates by grade used within the Department of Defense to develop military personnel budgets. They cover all elements in the military personnel appropriation except travel costs and allowances for support of free-world forces. Elements normally included in standard rates but not considered appropriate here were deducted: family separation and station allowances, and incentive and premium pays. Quarters allowances were also excluded and were calculated separately.

The government's contribution to social security for military employees poses particularly thorny problems when comparing the costs of

Table C-3. Estimated Average Annual Compensation-related Costs, Wage Board (Supervisor) Civilians, by Grade, 1978

Costs in 1978 dollars

Grade	Base pay	Overtime and holiday	Life insurance	Retirement	Miscel-laneous[a]	Total compensation-related costs
19	31,800	1,400	120	6,500	4,100	43,900
18	31,000	1,300	120	6,200	3,000	41,600
17	28,000	1,200	110	5,700	1,600	36,600
16	27,000	1,200	100	5,500	1,300	35,100
15	25,900	1,100	100	5,300	1,500	33,900
14	24,800	1,100	100	5,100	1,700	32,800
13	24,000	1,100	100	4,900	850	31,000
12	22,800	1,000	90	4,600	750	29,200
11	22,100	1,000	90	4,500	700	28,400
10	21,400	1,000	85	4,400	700	27,600
9	20,500	950	80	4,200	750	26,500
8	19,700	900	80	4,000	800	25,500
7	19,100	850	80	3,900	900	24,800
6	18,700	850	75	3,800	800	24,200
5	17,700	800	70	3,700	800	23,100
4	17,100	750	70	3,500	1,000	22,400
3	16,400	700	60	3,300	1,200	21,700
2	15,600	700	60	3,200	900	20,500
1	15,100	700	60	3,100	1,400	20,400

Source: Same as table C-1.
a. Includes health benefits, unemployment compensation, workmen's compensation, and terminal leave.

military and federal civilian employees. Military personnel are in an earnings category in which, on average, they can expect to contribute more than they will reap from the system (after adjustments for real growth). To make matters worse, federal civilians, who are not now required to participate in the system, often become eligible for social security either as a result of moonlighting or employment after they leave federal service. Since they make limited contributions over a relatively short period, these civilians can expect to get more out of the system than they put in. The force of the argument therefore suggests that the government contribution to social security for military personnel is not a "cost" to the government as such; indeed it can be argued that the cost of military personnel should be adjusted downward relative to the cost of federal civilians. However, because of the unsettled future of social security legislation and the sensitivity of the calculations to assumptions about future economic

Table C-4. Estimated Average Annual Compensation-related Costs, Wage Board (Leader) Civilians, by Grade, 1978

Costs in 1978 dollars

Grade	Base pay	Overtime and holiday	Life insurance	Retirement	Miscel- laneous[a]	Total compensation- related costs
15	22,500	1,300	90	4,500	800	29,200
14	21,100	1,100	90	4,300	1,000	27,600
13	19,700	900	· 80	4,000	850	25,500
12	19,400	900	80	4,000	800	25,200
11	19,200	900	80	3,900	700	24,800
10	18,300	850	70	3,700	700	23,600
9	17,200	800	70	3,500	700	22,300
8	16,400	750	70	3,300	750	21,300
7	16,200	750	60	3,300	800	21,100
6	15,300	700	60	3,100	800	20,000
5	14,900	700	60	3,100	800	19,600
4	13,500	600	50	2,700	850	17,700
3	12,700	600	50	2,600	1,000	17,000
2	12,000	550	50	2,500	1,050	16,200
1	10,500	500	50	2,100	2,000	15,200

Source: Same as table C-1.
a. Includes health benefits, unemployment compensation, workmen's compensation, and terminal leave.

conditions, we have chosen merely to ignore the government's contribution for military personnel in the cost calculations. This is all the more justified by heightening prospects that federal civilians will eventually be brought into the social security system.

Income tax adjustment represents an estimated "cost" to the federal government equivalent to the amount of additional cash income that would have to be provided to ensure the same take-home pay if allowances were taxable. Although this "cost" does not appear in the defense budget, it must be considered when comparing the cost of military and civilian personnel. The amount of tax savings on allowances is extremely variable depending on the recipient's tax bracket, the size of the allowances, and dependency status. The amounts shown are averages, estimated by the Department of Defense.

Basic allowance for quarters is the average of *cash* allowances provided to those who do not live in government housing. This assumes that increases or decreases in the number of military personnel would not affect occupancy of government-furnished housing.

Table C-5. Estimated Average Annual Compensation-related Costs, Wage Board (Nonsupervisor) Civilians, by Grade, 1978

Cost in 1978 dollars

Grade	Base pay	Overtime and holiday	Life insurance	Retirement	Miscel- laneous[a]	Total compensation- related costs
15	20,500	900	80	4,200	1,600	27,300
14	19,700	850	80	4,000	1,400	26,000
13	18,800	850	70	3,800	850	24,400
12	17,900	800	70	3,700	750	23,200
11	17,400	800	70	3,600	700	22,600
10	16,500	750	60	3,400	700	21,400
9	15,700	700	60	3,200	750	20,400
8	14,900	700	60	3,000	800	19,500
7	14,400	650	50	2,900	950	19,000
6	13,800	600	50	2,800	850	18,100
5	13,000	600	50	2,700	850	17,200
4	12,100	550	50	2,500	1,050	16,300
3	11,300	500	40	2,300	1,450	15,600
2	10,700	500	40	2,200	1,350	14,800
1	9,800	450	40	2,100	1,950	14,300

Source: Same as table C-1.

a. Includes health benefits, unemployment compensation, workmen's compensation, and terminal leave.

Retirement benefits are actuarially costed by the "entry age normal" method. Presupposing a fully funded retirement system, the method prescribes the computation of a fixed percentage of basic pay that, if set aside annually in an interest-bearing fund, accrues enough principal and interest to pay off future benefits as they come due. Assuming an annual real wage growth of 1.5 percent and a 2.5 percent real return on invested funds (in addition to various mortality and dependency data), the resulting fixed percentage of basic pay is about 36 percent for military personnel.

Miscellaneous costs include those associated with providing medical care, unemployment compensation, dependents' indemnity compensation, and GI Bill benefits. The costs of the individual components in this category are difficult to estimate accurately, particularly by grade. Estimates derived by the Department of Defense for the first three components were used. For GI Bill benefits, costs were distributed by grade in accordance with the assumption that the probability that the benefit would be used is related to grade as follows: 10 percent of those in grades E-5, E-6, O-3, and O-4 would use the benefits, while 20 percent of those in grades E-2 through E-4, E-7 through E-9, O-1, O-2, O-5, and O-6 would use the benefits. Under the current program, the government contributes $2 for each $1 contributed by the participants up to a limit of $5,400. Assuming a four-year period of contribution, annual per capita costs range between $130 and $270. Although per capita costs vary widely by grade within each component, the variations are largely self-canceling when aggregated into the miscellaneous category, and hence the result serves as a rough estimate of average costs by grade.

CIVILIAN PERSONNEL (TABLES C-2 THROUGH C-5). The elements constituting total compensation-related costs of civilian personnel were calculated as follows:

Base pay for civilians was derived from Department of Defense data. Variations exist between the services, particularly in regard to Wage Board employees. Defense-wide averages were used to estimate the base pay by grade for each category.

Overtime and holiday pay for each grade represents a weighted average by grade computed separately for general schedule and Wage Board employees obtained from Department of Defense data.

Life insurance costs are calculated as a proportion of base pay. The government pays one-third of the premium for participating members. The costs have been distributed by grade, assuming that participants are proportionately distributed by grade.

Retirement costs are calculated as a fixed percentage of base pay, assuming annual real wage growth of 1.5 percent and a 2.5 percent real return on invested funds. To fund the system fully under these economic assumptions, the government would have to set aside 20.4 percent of each employee's base pay, in addition to the employee's contribution of 7.0 percent.

Miscellaneous costs include health benefits, unemployment compensation, workmen's compensation, and terminal leave. Estimates were derived from data maintained by the military services. None of the categories can be considered highly accurate or reliable because accounting for such costs is not based on grade structure. Nonetheless, in the aggregate, the estimates are reasonable. Like life insurance, health benefit plans are based on voluntary contributions. The service estimates are derived by dividing total government health benefit contributions by civilian man-years, providing the same cost per member for each grade. Workmen's compensation is treated in a similar per capita fashion. The total workmen's compensation cost paid by the Labor Department for defense civilian employees for 1976 was divided by the number of employees to derive the per capita figure, inflated to 1978 levels. Obvious inaccuracies are inherent in this method, such as the implicit assumption that white-collar and blue-collar workers were equally likely to require workmen's compensation. Unemployment compensation payments, on the other hand, were weighted by the number of separations in each grade. This implicitly assumes that the number of separations provides a relative indication of the number of persons to be unemployed. Despite problems with this approach (separated GS-16s and GS-2s are probably not going to be unemployed in the same proportions) it is the only suitable one that available data allow.

Pipeline, Support, and Total Costs (Tables C-6 through C-8, 9, and 10)

In addition to the costs associated with personnel assigned to particular jobs in the Department of Defense are the costs associated with personnel turnover. Federal employees, particularly military personnel, are not permanently assigned to the same job or the same location. Incidental to the job reassignment process is the need to move personnel, their families, and their belongings, and, in the case of the military, to train replacements. Moreover, to ensure that units remain fully manned while military personnel are traveling between assignments or while they are patients in hospitals, the military services are provided extra people. These so-called pipeline costs were calculated as indicated below.

Training costs. For military personnel, the training categories included in the analysis were: recruit, officer acquisition (ROTC, service academies, officer candidate school, and the like), specialized skill, and professional development. Flight training costs, because of their high per capita cost and because they are distributed among a relatively small proportion of total military personnel, are not included. The costs within each category include the pay of students and instructors and direct operating expenses. Indirect costs associated with training were considered to be more relevant to the support cost category discussed below. Also included in training costs is travel associated with training courses.

Military training costs occurring at a specific grade were spread equally by grade over the actuarially determined remaining service time. Thus the cost of postgraduate education for an officer in grade O-3 was allocated (or capitalized) to all officer personnel above grade O-2. In the same fashion, leadership training for an enlisted man in grade E-5 was

Table C-6. Estimated Average Annual Pipeline Costs, Military Personnel, by Grade, 1978

Costs in 1978 dollars

Grade	Training cost	Travel cost	Other costs[a]	Total pipeline cost
Officer				
O-10	6,000	1,000	3,800	10,800
O-9	6,000	800	3,400	10,200
O-8	6,000	850	3,100	10,000
O-7	6,000	750	2,700	9,500
O-6	5,900	700	2,300	8,900
O-5	5,900	500	1,900	8,300
O-4	5,100	500	1,500	7,100
O-3	4,350	450	1,300	6,100
O-2	3,100	500	1,100	4,700
O-1	2,900	100	1,000	4,000
Warrant officer				
W-4	1,750	250	1,500	3,500
W-3	1,750	550	1,300	3,600
W-2	1,750	400	1,100	3,300
W-1	1,600	300	900	2,800
Enlisted				
E-9	1,400	350	1,300	3,100
E-8	1,400	300	1,200	2,900
E-7	1,400	250	1,000	2,700
E-6	1,350	250	900	2,500
E-5	1,350	250	700	2,300
E-4	1,350	250	600	2,200
E-3	1,100	10	550	1,700
E-2	1,100	10	500	1,600

Source: Based on Office of the Assistant Secretary of Defense (Manpower and Reserve Affairs), "Military Manpower Training Report for FY 1978" (1977; processed).

a. Other costs include those associated with extra personnel assigned to each service to offset time lost to units when personnel are in a travel status or hospital patients.

allocated to all men in grades E-5 through E-9 and W-1 through W-4. This causes higher military grades to absorb some of the costs of training provided years earlier and explains why training costs increase with grade. This allocation of training costs was done cross-sectionally rather than longitudinally; that is, instead of trying to predict changes in personnel grade levels over time, the current grade levels were assumed to be constant. This is equivalent to assuming a steady-state grade structure. The 1977 manpower distribution was the cross section used.

To illustrate the method, skill progression training is provided to officers commencing, on the average, at the O-2 grade level. The pay of

Table C-7. Estimated Average Annual Pipeline Costs, General Schedule Civilians, by Grade, 1978

Costs in 1978 dollars

Grade	Training cost	Travel cost	Total pipeline cost
18	1,700	700	2,400
17	1,700	600	2,300
16	1,700	600	2,300
15	1,100	500	1,600
14	900	450	1,350
13	750	350	1,100
12	650	350	1,000
11	600	300	900
10	550	250	800
9	500	250	750
8	450	200	650
7	400	200	600
6	350	150	500
5	300	150	450
4	150	100	250
3	100	10	110
2	100	10	110
1	50	10	60

Source: Based on U.S. Civil Service Commission, *Employee Training in the Federal Service, Fiscal Year 1973* (GPO, 1974), updated and adjusted for 1978 data.

instructors associated with such training, estimated at $45.8 million in fiscal 1977, was distributed uniformly among some 216,000 officers at grade O-2 and above. Student pay and direct operating expenses associated with this training were distributed similarly.

Civilian training costs could not be allocated in the same way as military costs for two reasons. First, unlike the military progression pattern, civilians can be hired and separated at any grade level. It therefore cannot be concluded that, say, GS-16s are a product of the training system and should absorb the cost of training a GS-11. Second, there is no clear distinction between management and labor analogous to the officer-enlisted categorization. Consequently, it would be inappropriate to allocate the cost of short-term training given to, say, GS-5s to the higher grades. For long-term training (over 120 days), on the other hand, the individual incurs an obligation to serve an additional period of time. Thus costs associated with this type of training were allocated to civilian grades in a manner similar to the military allocation. For training other than long-term, civilian training costs were allocated to the grade in

Table C-8. Estimated Annual Pipeline Costs, Wage Board Civilians, by Category and Grade, 1978

Costs in 1978 dollars

	Leader			Supervisor			Nonsupervisor		
Grade	Train-ing cost	Travel cost	Total pipeline cost	Train-ing cost	Travel cost	Total pipeline cost	Train-ing cost	Travel cost	Total pipeline cost
19	...	...	...	140	430	570	...	...	...
18	...	...	...	140	430	570	...	...	...
17	...	...	...	140	430	570	...	...	...
16	...	...	...	140	430	570	...	...	...
15	40	300	340	140	380	520	50	320	370
14	40	300	340	120	380	520	40	290	330
13	30	330	330	100	380	480	30	280	310
12	25	250	275	80	380	460	30	230	260
11	20	250	270	80	380	460	30	220	250
10	20	210	230	70	330	400	20	210	230
9	20	210	230	70	330	400	20	200	220
8	20	200	220	60	330	390	20	190	210
7	20	200	220	60	330	390	20	180	200
6	20	150	170	50	330	380	20	160	180
5	10	150	160	30	270	300	10	160	170
4	5	100	105	20	270	290	10	80	90
3	5	100	105	10	270	280	10	10	20
2	5	75	80	5	270	275	10	10	20
1	5	75	80	5	270	275	10	10	20

Source: Same as table C-7.

which the training is expected to occur. Since training data for general schedule civilians are available by groups of grades (for example, GS-1 to GS-4), but data for Wage Board civilians are available by totals only, the training costs imputed to the former should be considered more reliable when viewed by grade.

Travel costs. For military personnel, this category includes the costs of moving the military employee, his family, and their household goods when reassigned or separated. (The costs associated with moving a uniformed employee to the first-duty station—called accession travel— and those associated with moving an individual to and from a formal training course were included in the training cost category.) These costs were derived from data maintained by the military services. Travel costs for civilian employees are more difficult to estimate. Transportation costs for civilians are accounted for in disaggregated categories that are not

Table C-9. Estimated Average Annual Support Costs, Military and Civilian Personnel, by Grade, 1978

Costs in 1978 dollars

| Military | | General schedule | | Wage Board | | | | | |
| | | | | Supervisor | | Leader | | Nonsupervisor | |
Grade	Cost	Grade	Cost	Grade	Cost	Grade	Cost	Grade	Cost
Officer									
O-10	1,450	18	430	19	60	15	40	15	40
O-9	1,570	17	430	18	60	14	40	14	40
O-8	1,660	16	430	17	60	13	40	13	40
O-7	1,660	15	350	16	60	12	40	12	40
O-6	1,560	14	300	15	60	11	40	11	40
O-5	1,820	13	250	14	50	10	30	10	40
O-4	1,660	12	220	13	50	9	30	9	40
O-3	1,350	11	210	12	50	8	30	8	40
O-2	750	10	190	11	50	7	30	7	40
O-1	780	9	180	10	40	6	30	6	40
Warrant officer		8	160	9	40	5	30	5	30
W-4	1,380	7	150	8	40	4	30	4	30
W-3	1,440	6	130	7	40	3	30	3	30
W-2	1,440	5	120	6	40	2	30	2	30
W-1	1,160	4	70	5	40	1	30	1	30
Enlisted		3	60	4	40				
E-9	1,650	2	50	3	40				
E-8	1,650	1	40	2	30				
E-7	1,650			1	30				
E-6	1,560								
E-5	1,300								
E-4	1,060								
E-3	870								
E-2	830								

Source: See explanation in text.

a. Support includes training support and base operating support functions considered variable with personnel levels.

indexed by grade. Moreover, civilian transfers are not completely co-ordinated by the Department of Defense; both the Civil Service Commission and the General Services Administration are involved. The estimated costs by grade were based on the assumption that, on the average, the government will pay to move one federal civilian employee for every six military personnel. Moreover, after accounting for the differences in costs between civilian and military moves (for example, in the case of civilians, the government pays for real estate commissions

Table C-10. Estimated Average Total Costs by Grade, 1978[a]

Costs in 1978 dollars

Military		General schedule		Wage Board					
				Supervisor		Leader		Nonsupervisor	
Grade	Cost	Grade	Cost	Grade	Cost	Grade	Cost	Grade	Cost
Officer		GS-18	61,100	WS-19	44,500	WL-15	29,600	WG-15	27,700
O-10	95,700	GS-17	61,000	WS-18	42,200	WL-14	28,000	WG-14	26,400
O-9	87,700	GS-16	61,000	WS-17	37,200	WL-13	25,900	WG-13	24,800
O-8	81,100	GS-15	53,800	WS-16	35,700	WL-12	25,500	WG-12	23,500
O-7	70,300	GS-14	45,800	WS-15	34,500	WL-11	25,100	WG-11	22,900
O-6	62,100	GS-13	39,200	WS-14	33,400	WL-10	23,900	WG-10	21,700
O-5	51,900	GS-12	32,600	WS-13	31,500	WL-9	22,600	WG-9	20,700
O-4	42,900	GS-11	27,200	WS-12	29,700	WL-8	21,600	WG-8	19,800
O-3	36,800	GS-10	25,600	WS-11	28,900	WL-7	21,400	WG-7	19,200
O-2	29,000	GS-9	22,400	WS-10	28,000	WL-6	20,200	WG-6	18,300
O-1	21,900	GS-8	21,200	WS-9	26,900	WL-5	19,800	WG-5	17,400
Warrant officer		GS-7	18,700	WS-8	25,900	WL-4	17,800	WG-4	16,400
W-4	38,800	GS-6	17,200	WS-7	25,200	WL-3	17,100	WG-3	15,700
W-3	33,200	GS-5	15,400	WS-6	24,600	WL-2	16,300	WG-2	15,400
W-2	28,700	GS-4	13,600	WS-5	23,400	WL-1	15,300	WG-1	14,400
W-1	24,700	GS-3	11,800	WS-4	22,700				
Enlisted		GS-2	10,400	WS-3	22,000				
E-9	34,000	GS-1	9,500	WS-2	20,800				
E-8	30,200			WS-1	20,700				
E-7	26,400								
E-6	22,900								
E-5	19,400								
E-4	17,100								
E-3	14,600								
E-2	13,400								

Source: Tables C-1 through C-9.

a. Total costs include compensation, pipeline, and support costs.

and legal fees, exploratory trips to new locations, and unexpired leases), it was concluded that the average civilian move costs about four times as much as the average military move. Thus the average annual per capita cost imputed to civilians is estimated to be about two-thirds of the travel costs calculated for military personnel. This should be viewed as a rough estimate at best, but it constitutes only a small fraction of total civilian costs.

Other pipeline costs. Extra billets to offset time spent traveling or in hospital constituted 4.6 percent of 1977 military manning levels. Assuming that these costs are borne proportionately by grade, 4.6 percent of total compensation-related costs were allocated to each grade. Analogous costs were not calculated for civilian personnel since the military services do not explicitly plan for extra civilian billets for these purposes.

Support costs (table C-9). These costs include the variable component of base operating costs (feeding operations, recreation, welfare, and morale functions) for military personnel and training support costs for both military and civilian personnel. The base operating costs are based on estimates made by the military services. Training support costs for military and civilian personnel were allocated by the same method that was employed to allocate direct training costs. For civilians, it was assumed that the support cost per student man-hour is the same for military and civilian training.

Total costs (table C-10). This table assembles all the data on training, travel, support, and other costs to present average estimated costs by grade.

The Hay Point Linkage System

Several methods for comparing military and civilian grades were reviewed and the one developed by Hay Associates was selected for illustrative purposes. Theirs appeared to be the most detailed in its comparability factors and it is the most rigorously described method available. The comparison reflects an evaluation of job content by expertise and problem-solving skills required and by accountability. Points were assigned to a representative sample of military and civilian occupations. The median and the range of results for selected military grades and the relative positioning of equivalent civilian grades is shown in table C-11. Hay analysts concluded that the job content of the median

Table C-11. Comparison of High, Median, and Low Estimates of Job Content between Military Personnel and Federal Civilian Employees at Selected Grade Levels

Military grade and level of job content[a]	Relation of military grade to civilian grades				Point on percentage scale of military grade between civilian grades[b]	
	White-collar		Blue-collar		White-collar	Blue-collar
	Lower	Higher	Lower	Higher		
Officer						
Grade O-8						
Median	Above GS-18	...	...	...	57	...
Grade O-5						
High	GS-14	GS-15	...	...	64	...
Median	GS-14	GS-15	...	...	24	...
Low	GS-11	GS-14	...	...	41	...
Grade O-2						
High	GS-9	GS-11	...	...	73	...
Median	GS-9	GS-11	...	...	14	...
Low	GS-7	GS-9	...	...	58	...
Grade O-1						
High	GS-9	GS-11	...	...	5	...
Median	GS-7	GS-9	...	...	54	...
Low	GS-7	GS-9	...	...	9	...
Enlisted						
Grade E-7						
High	GS-7	GS-9	WS-9	WS-10	93	78
Median	GS-7	GS-9	WS-9	WS-10	18	37
Low	GS-5	GS-7	WS-9	...	87	...
Grade E-5						
High	GS-7	GS-9	WG-10	...	18	...
Median	GS-5	GS-7	WG-8	WG-10	26	80
Low	GS-3	GS-5	WG-8	WG-10	72	24
Grade E-3						
High	GS-3	GS-5	WG-6	WG-8	40	17
Median	GS-3	GS-5	WG-5	WG-6	13	79
Low	...	Below GS-3	...	Below WG-5	20	8

Source: Office of the Secretary of Defense, "Third Quadrennial Review of Military Compensation: Staff Studies and Selected Supporting Papers," vol. 8 (December 1976; processed).

a. "High" and "low" estimates represent highest and lowest values for military jobs sampled in that grade.

b. Expressed as a percentage of job-content difference between the civilian grades with next lower and next higher median job content. For example, median grade O-2 falls 14 percent of the way from median GS-9 to median GS-11. When a comparison falls on the exact grade, no difference is shown.

job for both military and civilians represented a good measure of central tendency.

Several items should be mentioned regarding the Hay method of job evaluations. First, they are based on written job specifications rather than on "desk-audits," which require interviews of employees actually holding the job. Barring this potential source of error, the Hay point system developed seems creditable. The Hay method is used worldwide by some 4,000 different organizations. Thus experience and reference data back up the Hay analysis. Second, the job evaluation process was conducted by a committee of nine persons who were neither defense nor civil service employees. One member was a retired military officer, but his evaluations did not reflect military bias when compared with other evaluations. Third, both the staff of the Civil Service Commission and the Pentagon's Quadrennial Review of Military Compensation assessed the job evaluations after completion. Of 140 military job evaluations, 9 were reappraised; and of 193 civilian jobs, 12 were reappraised. The QRMC evaluation of military jobs led to a downward adjustment of 5 jobs and an upward adjustment in 4 jobs—indicating balance in the influence of the QRMC on military job appraisal. On the other hand, the Civil Service Commission review of civilian jobs led to an upward adjustment in virtually all of the 12 civilian jobs reappraised—indicating some imbalance, either because the jobs were appraised low or because the CSC was more adamant in the upward revision process. Nonetheless, the small percentage of jobs reappraised indicates general satisfaction with the Hay methodology.

Discussions with persons conducting the Hay study provided further insights. First, the blue-collar jobs were apparently easier to appraise than the white-collar jobs. This is due to the specific nature of blue-collar work. Second, controversy in discussions following the study apparently centered around the highly visible grade O-8 and GS-18 comparisons. Far less argument occurred in the lower grades. For this reason (as well as the fact that relatively small amounts of money are involved) the GS-18 and O-8 comparison should be suppressed relative to the other grades. Finally, the study did include various military jobs (infantry unit commander, air operations officer) in the data base. This made it more representative in the military categories than previous linkage systems.

The job occupations selected (140 military, 193 civilian) were based on several criteria. They were chosen from those jobs with the largest numbers of incumbents, and, where possible, for those jobs allowing comparability (for example, military police and civilian policeman).

Table C-12. Estimated Median Military Costs Relative to High, Median, and Low Estimates for Equivalent Civilian Grades, 1978

Costs in 1978 dollars

Military grade	Compensation-related costs			Compensation plus pipeline			Total costs[a]		
	Military median	General schedule	Wage Board	Military median	General schedule	Wage Board	Military median	General schedule	Wage Board
O-8[a]	69,400	69,700	...	78,700	72,100	...	81,100	72,500	...
O-5	41,800	49,000	...	46,600	50,500	...	51,900	50,900	...
		45,900	...		47,300	...		47,700	...
		33,500	...		34,600	...		34,800	...
O-2	23,500	24,900	...	27,900	25,800	...	29,000	25,900	...
		22,100	...		22,900	...		23,100	...
		20,000	...		20,700	...		20,800	...
O-1	17,100	21,700	...	20,800	22,500	...	21,900	22,600	...
		19,800	...		20,500	...		20,700	...
		18,200	...		18,900	...		19,000	...
E-7	22,100	21,200	27,400	24,600	22,000	27,700	26,400	22,100	27,800
		18,500	26,900		19,200	27,300		19,400	27,300
		17,500	26,500		18,200	26,900		18,300	26,900
E-5	15,800	18,500	21,400	17,900	19,200	21,700	19,400	19,400	21,700
		15,600	21,000		16,100	21,300		16,300	21,300
		13,900	20,000		14,300	20,300		14,400	20,300
E-3	12,100	12,900	18,300	13,600	13,100	18,600	14,600	13,200	18,600
		12,000	17,900		12,200	18,100		12,300	18,100
		11,200	17,100		11,200	17,200		11,300	17,300

Source: Derived from information contained in U.S. Office of the Secretary of Defense, "Third Quadrennial Review of Military Compensation," vol. 8 (1976; processed), and from data in tables C-1 through C-11.

a. Total costs include compensation, pipeline, and support costs.

b. For grade O-8, only civilian median estimates are provided. High and low equivalents are omitted because the number of personnel in this grade is too small to permit even rough estimates.

Some jobs were chosen because they appeared across grades (that is, at the E-3, E-5, E-7 levels). Again, the O-8 and GS-18 jobs did not allow for the application of these criteria in any depth.

The overall appraisal is that if the job specifications are indicative of job content, then the Hay points seem fairly unbiased indicators of job comparability in all grades compared with the possible exception of the O-8 level, where information is simply inadequate for a high level of confidence.

Cost Comparison

Table C-12, which compares the total costs of equivalent military and civilian grades, is based on the relationship developed in tables C-1 through C-11. Linear interpolation was used to derive the civilian equivalents for all grades except grade O-8. In that case a curvilinear extrapolation of the direct cost trends from grades GS-7 to GS-18 was extended to a point equivalent to the grade O-8 level Hay point. Because of the large extrapolation required, the grade O-8 civilian equivalent is tentative.

At the highest grades a special note of caution is appropriate. In these grades, particularly at the officer grade O-7 through O-10 levels and the civilian GS-17 and GS-18 levels, there are few individuals relative to the total manpower force. This small sample size could distort the cost figures in these grades. There are, for instance, less than twenty grade WS-18s in the Department of Defense.